PRAISE FOR

CULTURE OF COMPLAINT

"A SMALL GEM...I can't wait for the sequel."
—Herbert Mitgang, *New York Times*

"THIS IS ONE HELL OF A GOOD BOOK."
—George V. Higgins, *Chicago Sun-Times*

"HIS LENS IS CLEAR...a vivid performance...rich and absorbing."
—Linda Bradley Salamon, *New York Times Book Review*

"A WONDERFUL HANDHELD-CAMERA TOUR OF THE DUMB
ZONES OF AMERICAN LIFE."
—*Artforum*

"WHAT GOOD SENSE. How bracing. How cathartic....Hughes
writes like George Bernard Shaw on a good night."
—*Los Angeles Times Book Review*

"His particular gift is to understand the foibles of both sides as
symptoms of a single malaise."
—Henry Louis Gates, Jr., *The New Yorker*

"Hughes's book is a lesson in balanced commentary."
—*Boston Globe*

"AN INESCAPABLY QUOTABLE BIBLE OF INTELLECTUAL
COMMON SENSE."
—David Denby, *New Republic*

"ROBERT HUGHES IS MAD AS HELL AND...when Hughes gets
angry he is at his best."
—Robert L. Pincus, *San Diego Union-Tribune*

"BRILLIANT MOCKING CULTURAL CRITICISM."
—Alfred Kazin, *The New York Review of Books*

ALSO BY ROBERT HUGHES

Barcelona (1992)
Frank Auerbach (1990)
Nothing if Not Critical (1990)
Lucian Freud (1988)
The Fatal Shore (1987)
The Shock of the New (1981, 1991)
Heaven and Hell in Western Art (1969)
The Art of Australia (1966)
Donald Friend (1965)

ROBERT HUGHES, *Time* magazine's long-standing art critic, is the bestselling author of nine books including *The Shock of the New*, *Barcelona*, and *The Fatal Shore*, winner of the National Book Award. His most recent award, the international El Brusi prize for literature and communications, was given by the Olimpiada Cultural in Barcelona in 1992.

Culture of Complaint

THE FRAYING OF AMERICA

Robert Hughes

WARNER BOOKS

A Time Warner Company

This Warner Books edition is published by arrangement with Oxford University Press, Inc., 200 Madison Ave., New York, NY 10016, and the New York Public Library.

Warner Books, Inc., 1271 Avenue of the Americas, New York, NY 10020

Ⓦ A Time Warner Company

Printed in the United States of America
First Warner Books Printing: September 1994
10 9 8 7 6 5 4 3 2 1

Library of Congress Cataloging-in-Publication Data
Hughes, Robert, 1938-
    Culture of complaint : the fraying of America / Robert Hughes. --Warner Books ed.
      p. cm.
    Includes bibliographical references (p.).
    ISBN 0-446-67034-0
    1. Arts and society--United States--History--20th century.
  2. Popular culture--United States. I. Title.
  [NX180.S6H85 1994]
  700'.1'0309730904--dc20   93-41839
                                                  CIP

Cover design by Julia Kushnirsky
Cover photograph by Melissa Hyden

For Elizabeth Sifton

Contents

Introduction, ix

Lecture 1
Culture and the Broken Polity, 1

Lecture 2
Multi-Culti and Its Discontents, 85

Lecture 3
Moral in Itself:
Art and the Therapeutic Fallacy, 155

Notes, 205

Introduction

*T*HIS BOOK GROWS out of the series of lectures I was invited to give under the auspices of Oxford University Press and the New York Public Library at the Library in January 1992. Already, for several years, the clouded issues of "political correctness," "multiculturalism," the politicization of the arts and so forth had been moving from academe, the artworld and the cultural magazines into American popular journalism, creating, on the whole, more heat and fumes than light. I thought it might be interesting and perhaps worthwhile to take a look at them from the point of view of a practicing writer, neither an academic nor an American citizen, but with one leg in history and the other in the visual arts. This involved walking across a number of social minefields, and speculating about areas which are not my speciality, such as education in a country in which I did not grow up,

and politics in a state where I cannot vote; for this I make no
apology. After twenty-two years in the U.S., much of it still
seems highly exotic to me, most of all the peculiarly exacerbated relations between culture and morality which were, in
large part, the subject of the lectures and of this book. I hope
the reader will not misconstrue this as anti-Americanism, or as
the unearned condescension of a foreigner. Next to Australia,
America is the place I know and love best, and I feel a visceral
attachment to it by now. That should be plain from the ensuing pages.

A one-hour lecture is short, five thousand words at the
most. On finishing the series, I felt dissatisfied at having
touched on a variety of matters without being able to dilate
on them. Immediately afterwards, the text of the first two
lectures was abridged into a cover story for the February 3
issue of *Time,* "The Fraying of America." (The third lecture
was published in full by the *New York Review of Books;* once
again, I must thank its editor, Robert Silvers, and my editors
at *Time,* Walter Isaacson and Christopher Porterfield, for their
encouragement, enthusiasm and hard work in turning the
spoken word into the word on the page.) The public response
this evoked was so large that I decided to give the argument
its length, and the result is this book. Written between the
spring and fall of 1992, it contains many references to events
which were not touched on in the original lectures, because
they had not yet happened. Chief among these was the victory
of the Democratic party under Bill Clinton, in a Presidential
election which was, to no small extent, a referendum on many
of the issues referred to in my original text.

My debts to others, in conversation, are many and large.
I cannot list them all, but I owe particular ones to Arthur

Schlesinger (whose own recent book, *The Disuniting of America*, says much of what I say but said it earlier and better); to Gilbert T. Sewell of the *Social Studies Review*, for supplying me with a copy of that singular document, *The Portland Baseline Essays*; to Edward Saïd; and to David Rieff. And as always, to my beloved wife Victoria Hughes, and her perfect commonsense.

LECTURE 1
Culture and the Broken Polity

*J*UST OVER FIFTY YEARS AGO, the poet W. H. Auden achieved what all writers envy: a prophecy that came true. It's embedded in a long work called *For the Time Being: A Christmas Oratorio,* where Herod enlarges on the distasteful task of massacring the Innocents. He doesn't want to, because he is at heart a liberal. But still, he says, if that child is allowed to get away,

"One doesn't have to be a prophet to predict the consequences . . .

"Reason will be replaced by Revelation . . . Knowledge will degenerate into a riot of subjective visions—feelings in the solar plexus induced by undernourishment, angelic images generated by fever or drugs, dream warnings inspired by the sound of falling water. Whole cosmogonies will be created out of some forgotten personal resentment, complete epics written in private languages, the daubs of schoolchildren ranked above the greatest masterpieces . . .

"Idealism will be replaced by Materialism . . . Diverted from its normal outlet in patriotism and civic or family pride, the need of the masses for some visible Idol to worship will be driven into totally unsociable channels where no education can reach it. Divine honours will be paid to shallow depressions in the earth, domestic pets, ruined windmills, or malignant tumours.

"Justice will be replaced by Pity as the cardinal human virtue, and all fear of retribution will vanish. Every corner-boy will congratulate himself: 'I'm such a sinner that God has come down in person to save me.' Every crook will argue: 'I like committing crimes. God likes forgiving them. Really the world is admirably arranged.' The New Aristocracy will consist exclusively of hermits, bums and permanent invalids. The Rough Diamond, the Consumptive Whore, the bandit who is good to his mother, the epileptic girl who has a way with animals will be the heroes and heroines of the New Tragedy, when the general, the statesman, and the philosopher have become the butt of every farce and satire."

What Herod saw was America in the late 80s and early 90s. A polity obsessed with therapies and filled with distrust of formal politics; skeptical of authority and prey to superstition; its political language corroded by fake pity and euphemism. Like late Rome, unlike the early republic, in its long imperial reach, in the corruption and verbosity of its senators, in its reliance on sacred geese (those feathered ancestors of our own pollsters and spin-doctors) and in its submission to senile, deified emperors controlled by astrologers and extravagant wives. A culture which has replaced gladiatorial games, as a means of pacifying the mob, with hi-tech wars on television that cause immense slaughter and yet leave the Mesopotamian satraps in full power over their wretched subjects.

Unlike Caligula, the emperor does not appoint his horse consul; he puts him in charge of the environment, or appoints him to the Supreme Court. Mainly it is women who object, for due to the prevalence of mystery-religions the men are off in the woods, affirming their manhood by sniffing one another's armpits and listening to third-rate poets rant about the moist, hairy satyr that lives inside each one of them. Those who crave the return of the Delphic sibyl get Shirley MacLaine, and a 35,000-year-old Cro-Magnon warrior named Ramtha takes up residence inside a blonde housewife on the West Coast, generating millions upon millions of cult dollars in seminars, tapes and books.

Meanwhile, artists vacillate between a largely self-indulgent expressiveness and a mainly impotent politicization, and the contest between education and TV—between argument and conviction by spectacle—has been won by television, a medium now more debased in America than ever before. Even its popular arts, once the wonder and delight of the world, have decayed; there was a time, within the memory of some of us, when American popular music was full of exaltation and pain and wit, and appealed to grown-ups. Today, instead of the raw intensity of Muddy Waters or the virile inventiveness of Duke Ellington, we have Michael Jackson, and from George Gershwin and Cole Porter we are down to illiterate spectaculars about cats or the fall of Saigon. The great American form of rock-'n'-roll has become over-technologized and run through the corporate grinder, until it is 95 percent synthetic.

For the young, more and more, entertainment sets educational standards and creates "truth" about the past. Millions of Americans, especially young ones, imagined that the "truth" about the Kennedy assassination resides in Oliver Stone's vivid lying film *JFK,* with its paranoid elevation of a discredited New Orleans prosecutor into a political hero beset by an evil, omnipresent military establishment that murdered Kennedy to keep us in Vietnam. How many of them saw anything wrong with Stone's frequent claim that he was "creating a counter-myth" to the Warren Commission's findings, as though one's knowledge of the past equated with the propagation of myth? Hollywood's treatment of history used not to matter—that harmless gadzookery about Louis XV, or 'pon-my-soulery about Lord Nelson, or devotional claptrap about Jesus. But in a time of docudramas and simulations, when the difference between TV and real events is more and more blurred—not by accident, but as deliberate policy from the bosses of electronic media—such exercises fall into a mushy, anxious context of suspended disbelief that old Hollywood pseudo-history never had.

And then, because the arts confront the sensitive citizen with the difference between good artists, mediocre ones and absolute duffers, and since there are always more of the last two than the first, the arts too must be politicized; so we cobble up critical systems to show that although we know what we mean by the quality of the environment, the idea of "quality" in aesthetic experience is little more than a paternalist fiction designed to make life hard for black, female and homosexual artists, who must henceforth be judged on their ethnicity, gender and medical condition rather than the merits of their work.

As a maudlin reaction against excellence spreads to the

arts, the idea of *aesthetic* discrimination is tarred with the brush of *racial* or *gender* discrimination. Few take a stand on this, or point out that in matters of art "elitism" does not mean social injustice or even inaccessibility. The self is now the sacred cow of American culture, self-esteem is sacrosanct, and so we labor to turn arts education into a system in which no-one can fail. In the same spirit, tennis could be shorn of its elitist overtones: you just get rid of the net.

Since our new-found sensitivity decrees that only the victim shall be the hero, the white American male starts bawling for victim status too. Hence the rise of cult therapies which teach that we are all the victims of our parents: that whatever our folly, venality, or outright thuggishness, we are not to be blamed for it, since we come from "dysfunctional families"— and, as John Bradshaw, Melody Beattie and other gurus of the twelve-step program are quick to point out on no evidence whatsoever, 96 percent of American families are dysfunctional. We have been given imperfect role models, or starved of affection, or beaten, or perhaps subjected to the goatish lusts of Papa; and if we don't think we have, it is only because we have repressed the memory and are therefore in even more urgent need of the quack's latest book.

The number of Americans who were abused as children and hence absolved from all blame for anything they might now do is more or less equal to the number who, a few years ago, had once been Cleopatra or Henry VIII. Thus the ether is now jammed with confessional shows in which a parade of citizens and their role-models, from Latoya Jackson to Roseanne Barr, rise to denounce the sins of their parents, real or imagined. Not to be aware of a miserable childhood is prima facie evidence, in the eyes of Recovery, of "denial"—

the assumption being that everyone had one, and is thus a potential source of revenue. The cult of the abused Inner Child has a very important use in modern America: it tells you that personal grievance transcends political utterance, and that the upward production curve of maudlin narcissism need not intersect with the descending spiral of cultural triviality. Thus the pursuit of the Inner Child has taken over just at the moment when Americans ought to be figuring out where their Inner Adult is, and how that disregarded oldster got buried under the rubble of pop psychology and specious short-term gratification. We imagine a Tahiti inside ourselves, and seek its prelapsarian inhabitant: everyone his own Noble Savage.

If the Inner Child doesn't let you off the hook, the embrace of redemption will. It used to be said that there are no second acts in American lives. That was before TV started burning out our memory-cells. The public life of America today is largely made up of second acts, and has become an unconvincing parody of the original promise of America as a place where anyone, relieved of the burdens of the Old World, could make a fresh start. I remember feeling some qualms fifteen years ago when Charles Colson, one of the minor Washington villains of the Watergate years, announced at the very gate of the minimum-security prison that he had seen the light of Christ and been born again. Surely Americans won't swallow this? But they did. Even David Duke said he was reborn from Nazism into the brotherhood of Christ—and thousands of people believed him. Next, Robert Maxwell's family will tell his aggrieved bankers and former employees that he was moral at the last, and died from a bungled attempt at self-baptism by total immersion. With so many crooks queuing up to be washed in the blood of the Lamb, it's no wonder that the poor creature is looking a bit pale.

The vulgarity of confessional culture is stupefying, but "vulgarity" has ceased to matter in America: it is no longer a term of rebuke, since it is now completely identified with democracy. The classic definition of vulgarity was inappropriate self-exposure. It contrasted the "mob"—the *vulgus*, all emotion and no reason, easily manipulated and cheaply satisfied—to the reserved patrician who maintained power through distance and an unshakeable code. "I could be well moved, if I were as you," says Shakespeare's Julius Caesar, reflecting on his inferiors, men who are "flesh and blood, and apprehensive"—

> Yet in the number I do know but one
> That unassailable holds on his rank
> Unshaked of motion; and that I am he
> Let me a little show it . . .

This idea of distinction is long gone; no American would admit to it, even if he or she secretly yearned for it. The longing for aristocracy is metabolized as a more "democratic" hunger for celebrity. Millions dream of celebrity who never think of aristocracy. There goes the celeb, and there, perhaps, go I. And celebrity in America today is a caterwauling freakshow.

Television has contributed hugely to this. To be on TV, if you *believe* in TV, is to break through the ceiling, to become realer than real. Many think that vulgarity is the opposite of snobbery; but snobbery is only a form of the vulgar. The real opposite of vulgarity is dignity. But this hardly matters on

TV, which prefers emotion to dignity and positively loathes reserve.

All one needs, then, to reconcile the dreams of celebrity with the loss of dignity is a belief that self-exposure confers distinction. That consensus has arrived, in the immense social fallout from American pop-therapeutics. The "recovery" movement, with its prattle of self-esteem, its metaphors of addiction and Inner Children, its obsession with buried (or induced) memories and its often trivial approach to "victim- ization" and "oppression," was made for TV all along. There has always been a vulgarity of aggression, based on sex and violence; now American mass culture has a vulgarity of thera- peutics, undreamt of twenty years ago. Enter a form which sometimes does help suffering people, and sometimes turns them into a freakshow: confessional TV, group therapy on prime time, with each encounter poked and prodded along by an emcee known to millions by his or her first name: Oprah and Sally and Phil, Geraldo and Maury, with ten more confession-shows trying to break into the network and cable slots every season.

There are wide differences between the shows, of course. The air of sanctimonious concern that envelops Geraldo Ri- vera like a flasher's raincoat is absent from bustling Oprah Winfrey or the firm, maternal Sally Jesse Raphael. But the common virtue of the format, from the producers' viewpoint, is its rockbottom cheapness. No actors or even scriptwriters need be paid. Raphael's show gets five crates of mail a day, much of it consisting of applications from people who long to bare their wounds to her. If they could spare the cash, they would probably pay to do it. Part of the shows' allure is that audience and guests are the same people, as in a religious revival meeting.

The shows are mocked and loved for their themes: Lesbian Nuns, Transvestites Who Live with Their Mothers, Women Whose Breasts Are Too Big, a row of men with large penises (though not on open parade) discussing with Sally the topic "Does Size Make a Difference?" and, one climactic afternoon on the Oprah Winfrey Show, "People Who Eat Their Feet." No subject is too bizarre to be addressed in public.

There is (as yet) no such thing in American academe as a chair of talkshowology, but if there were one James Robert Parish, a Californian entertainment writer, should get it: in researching a book on the trend, he watched over 1,000 hours of confession shows. This heroic feat left him skeptical about the future. Novel guests and exotic dysfunctions are getting harder to find. Producers squabble over the available ones like coyotes over tacos, sometimes with results that no satirist could improve on: recently *US* Magazine reported how Laura Thorpe of Bloomfield, N.M., who had cut out her breast implants with a disposable razor, was flown to New York with her three kids and unemployed husband by Sally Jesse Raphael's staff, pirated out of the hotel by Maury Povich's, thrust on Povich's camera dazed with medication, and then left stranded without airfare home by Raphael's irate producers. Competition can only breed more folly and sensationalism—and there is a full-time confession-talk cable channel in the offing as well. Unsurprisingly, Parish opines that the talks "are bringing down the cultural and intellectual level of what appears on television." The afternoon soaps weren't exactly Plato's Symposium, but at this level every inch counts.

Moreover, Parish warns, if you find the American afternoon's obsessive spritzing of sorrow, pity, voyeurism and pseudotherapy a bit hard to take, just wait. In quest of more spectacular psychodramas, the blurt-talks will move from the studio to the home. Hidden cameras will be there, with consent of the parties. "The next step will be, 'Can we have our cameras there when you invite your daughter over to discuss why you threw her out?' "

If this sounds familiar, a bad dream from the far distant past of TV, it is. Some twenty years ago PBS ran a real-life series called *An American Family*, an armpit-close documentation of the daily doings of some folks called, with divine irony, the Louds. It made a starlet of the oldest son, a gay named Lancelot.

It never developed a big audience. Nevertheless it was the direct ancestor of today's confessional talkies, and its own ancestry would seem to have lain outside the network world— in Andy Warhol's Factory, with its ever-spooling cassettes.

Those who remember sitting through Warhol's *Chelsea Girls* in the '60s will find the tone of talk-show confession in the '90s eerily familiar. Both are propelled by an inescapable fact of our culture, which is that people will do and say anything, anything at all, in order to get on camera, to be noticed and recorded by television: TV now defines their sense of reality to such an extent that only it can validate their lives and give a short flash of meaning to what they fear may be meaningless. All you need be is yourself, while the camera is on you.

In any case, the urge to confess in public is much older than Oprah, or Warhol movies, or TV. Like much else that is truly fundamental to American culture, it came here with the Puritans and it has never gone away. It has always been associated with "enthusiasm"—gut religious irrationality, as with Wesleyan Methodism in the eighteenth century or peasant Anabaptists in the sixteenth. Such rituals were totally different from the more ordered forms of confession and forgiveness that came with Roman Catholicism and High Church Anglicanism. The Catholic discloses his sins to the priest (and no one else) in a whisper. The penitent at the tent meeting falls raving to the ground, revealing her sins to the Lord, the pastor and the rest of the congregation. Then she is borne up, reinforced by other ex-sinners in a transport of therapeutic sharing. Forgiveness comes, not from authority, but from mutuality. The delight of confession prolongs the pleasure of sin.

But of course, in the end, there is no sin. Only our parents sinned, in abusing us. If we think we remember that, it happened. And perhaps they were not to blame, since their parents abused them. Under the sign of vulgar therapeutics, the moral buck is endlessly passed back to people who, being dead or absent, can't reply. The end result is that, while Washington resounds with presidential exhortations to get tough on crime, in California we can murder our parents for their money with relative impunity, as long as we get a lawyer who can pull the strings of cheap talk-show empathy. "What they did is not the issue," claimed Erik Menendez's attorney, Leslie Abramson, "It's why they did it. These boys were not responsible for who they turned out to be. They were just little children being molded." Purchase the usual expert witnesses, and suffer the little molded ones to get a mistrial. Not responsible, not responsible: these words seem destined for the courthouse pediment. But here we pass from vulgarity to obscenity. The bizarre effect of the assumption that previous suffering, real or (in the Menendez case) merely alleged, without a scintilla of evidence, is to return us to eye-for-an-eye law, Hollywood Hammurabi—in the name of "mercy." If I can say that Papa sexually abused me, I can be excused for blasting him to mincemeat twenty years later. This notion of mercy legitimates all revenge, however brutal. Thus when a deranged black man runs amok killing commuters at random with an automatic pistol on a New York train, the lawyer William Kunstler can unblushingly enter a "rage defense" on his behalf; white racism had enraged him, so that law no longer applies. White society is to blame for the deaths of its innocent members. The killer is merely—how to put it?— a delayed historical reaction, deserving more pity than his victims.

The all-pervasive claim to victimhood tops off America's long-cherished culture of therapeutics. To seem strong may only conceal a rickety scaffolding of denial, but to be vulnerable is to be invincible. Complaint gives you power—even when it's only the power of emotional bribery, of creating previously unnoticed levels of social guilt. Plead not guilty, and it's off with your head. The shifts this has produced may be seen everywhere, and their curious tendency is to make the "right" and the "left" converge. Consider the recent form of discussion of sexual issues, which revolve more and more around victimization. Pro-lifers borrow feminist lingo to call abortion "surgical rape" (never mind that it is a wholly voluntary act).

Meanwhile, the new orthodoxy of feminism is abandoning the image of the independent, existentially responsible woman in favor of woman as helpless victim of male oppression— treat her as equal before the law, and you are compounding her victimization. Conservatives have been delighted to cast their arguments in the same terms of victimology, with the difference that, for them, what produces victims is feminism itself, in league with the opportunist phallus. In *Enemies of Eros* (1990), the antifeminist writer Maggie Gallagher claims that "A man exploits a woman every time he uses her body for sexual pleasure when he is unwilling to accept the full burden of paternity." She "may consent fully, knowledgeably, enthusiastically to her exploitation. This does not change the nature of the transaction." Almost precisely the view of the feminist Andrea Dworkin—sex between men and women is always rape. "Physically the woman in intercourse," writes this extremist, "is a space invaded, a literal territory occupied literally; occupied even if there has been no resistance; even if the occupied woman said, 'Yes, please, yes hurry, yes more.' "[1] Such grotesquely expanded views of criminal assault reduce women to victims without free will, deprived equally of the power of assent or of denial, mere dolls tossed around in the ideological flurries of feminist extremism. "Viewing 'yes' as a sign of true consent," wrote the Harvard Law School professor Susan Estrich, "is misguided." Everything is rape until proven otherwise.

And rape, for those persuaded by the victim-feminist law professor Catherine McKinnon, includes depictions of rape. McKinnon is the kind of American lawyer who, in seventeenth-century Massachusetts, might have been scrutinizing old women for warts, polyps and other forensic evidence of witchery. She believes symbols and representations *are* realities; her tendentious and strident book *Only Words*, 1993, argues that in pornography there is no difference between word and deed, so that vile sex films are rape and should be punished as such. Men, in Professor McKinnon's dyspeptic and sexist view, are merely instinctual beasts, on whom pornographic speech acts as the word "kill" acts on a trained Doberman. Ten years ago, it might have been assumed that radical feminists and ultraconservatives were broadcasting on different bands: not today.

In these and a dozen other ways we create an infantilized culture of complaint, in which Big Daddy is always to blame and the expansion of rights goes on without the other half of citizenship—attachment to duties and obligations. To be infantile is a regressive way to defy the stress of corporate culture: Don't tread on me, I'm vulnerable. The emphasis is on the subjective: how we feel about things, rather than what we think or can know. The problems of this inward-turning were sketched long ago by Goethe, speaking to Eckermann. "Epochs which are regressive, and in the process of dissolution, are always subjective, whereas the trend in all progressive epochs is objective. . . . Every truly excellent endeavour turns from within toward the world, as you see in the great epochs which were truly in progression and aspiration, and which were all objective in nature."

II

As Auden saw, what this culture likes is the twin fetishes of victimhood and redemption. The Puritans saw themselves, with reason, as the victims of persecution, sent forth to create a theocratic state whose virtues would transcend the evils of the Old World and thus redeem the fall of European man. The sublime radical experiment of American democracy— and it is worth remembering that although we tend to think of America as perpetually new, the fall of despotisms leaves its form of government older and more continuous than any in Europe, older than the French Revolution and much older than British parliamentary democracy—was to break the status of colonial victim, and create a secular state in which self-evident rights would be continuously expanded in the interest of equality.

There has always been a friction between the remains of the Puritan ideology of a hierarchy of the virtuous under the immutable eye of God, and the later, revolutionary, 18th-century American conception of continuous secular development towards equality of rights which were inherent in man and not merely granted by government. This friction never seems to vanish; we still feel it today. It was foreseen in 1835 by Alexis de Tocqueville, in *Democracy in America*:

> Men will never establish any equality with which they will be contented. . . . When inequality of condition is the common law of society, the most marked inequalities do not strike the eye; when everything is nearly on the same level, the slightest are marked enough to hurt it. Hence the desire for equality always becomes more insatiable in proportion as equality is more complete.

Such was the view of a visitor from the Old World, so class-bound that he thought equality was "the common law" in a country which was still a slave state. We can't imagine sharing his lofty elitism, but Tocqueville did have a point. The fundamental temper of America tends towards an existential ideal which can probably never be reached, but can never be discarded: equal rights to variety, to construct your life as you see fit, to choose your traveling companions. This has always been a heterogeneous country and its cohesion, whatever cohesion it has, can only be based on mutual respect. There never was a core America in which everyone looked the same, spoke the same language, worshipped the same gods and believed the same things. Even before the Europeans arrived, American Indians were constantly at one another's throats. America is a construction of mind, not of race or inherited class or ancestral territory.

These things, I know, have been said before, but their obvious truth is why America has always seemed marvelous to foreigners like me. It does not mean that America has a monopoly on freedom, or even that its models of freedom are exportable everywhere in the world. But it is a creed born from immigration, from the jostling of scores of tribes who become American to the extent to which they can negotiate accommodations with one another. These negotiations succeed unevenly, and often fail: you only need to glance at the history of racial relations to know that.

It is too simple to say that America is, or ever was, a melting pot. But it is also too simple to say none of its contents actually melted. No single metaphor can do justice to the complexity of cultural crossing and perfusion in America. American mutuality has no choice but to live in recognition of difference. But it is destroyed when those differences get raised into cultural ramparts. People once used a dead metaphor—"balkanization"—to evoke the splitting of a field into sects, groups, little nodes of power. Now, on the dismembered corpse of Yugoslavia, whose "cultural differences" (or, to put it plainly, archaic religious and racial lunacies) have been set free by the death of Communism, we see what that stale figure of speech once meant and now means again. A Hobbesian world: the war of all on all, locked in blood-feud and theocratic hatred, the *reductio ad insanitatem* of America's mild and milky multiculturalism. What imperial rule, what Hapsburg tyranny or slothful dominion of Muscovite apparatchiks, would not be preferable to this? Against this ghastly background, so remote from American experience since the Civil War, we now have our own conservatives promising a "culture war," while ignorant radicals orate about "separatism." They cannot know what demons they are frivolously invoking. If they did, they would fall silent in shame.

Two hundred and sixty million people make up the same country, but this does not mean that they are all the same kind of people, with the same beliefs and mores. The fact remains that America is a collective work of the imagination whose making never ends, and once that sense of collectivity and mutual respect is broken the possibilities of Americanness begin to unravel. If they are fraying now, it is because the politics of ideology has for the last twenty years weakened and in some areas broken the traditional American genius for consensus, for getting along by making up practical compromises to meet real social needs.

Through the 80s, this happened with depressing regularity on both sides of American party politics. Instead of common ground, we got demagogues urging that there is only one path to virtuous American-ness: palaeo-conservatives like Jesse Helms and Pat Robertson who think this country has one single ethic, neo-conservatives who create an exaggerated bogey called multiculturalism—as though Western culture itself was ever anything *but* multi, living by its eclecticism, its power of successful imitation, its ability to absorb "foreign" forms and stimuli!—and pushers of political correctness who would like to see grievance elevated into automatic sanctity.

In society as in farming, monoculture works poorly. It

exhausts the soil. The social richness of America, so striking to the foreigner, comes from the diversity of its tribes. Its capacity for cohesion, for some spirit of common agreement on what is to be done, comes from the willingness of those tribes not to elevate their cultural differences into impassable barriers and ramparts, not to fetishize their "African-ness" or *Italianitá,* which make them distinct, at the expense of their Americanness, which gives them a vast common ground. Reading America is like scanning a mosaic. If you only look at the big picture, you do not see its parts—the distinct glass tiles, each a different color. If you concentrate only on the tiles, you cannot see the picture.

We have entered a period of intolerance which combines, as it sometimes does in America, with a sugary taste for euphemism. This conjuction fosters events that go beyond the wildest dreams of satire—if satire existed in America any more; perhaps the reason for its weakness is that reality has superseded it. Take, for example, the battle for victims' rights recently staged in Betty's Oceanview Diner in Berkeley, California, and reported with a degree of morose gusto by Nat Hentoff in the *Village Voice.*[2]

There, one morning in 1991, a waitperson named Barbara, who afterwards refused to reveal her surname, saw a journalist sitting on his own and perusing a magazine article on the Bill of Rights by the same Nat Hentoff. But the magazine was *Playboy,* and so Barbara Somethingperson refused to serve him breakfast, claiming that she was "appalled and shocked," that the very sight of *Playboy* was a form of vicarious rape, sexual harassment in the workplace, a threat to women's self-esteem, and so on.

She and the manager asked him to leave. So the wretched

scribe, who really only wanted a muffin and maybe some OJ, not a civil rights confrontation, retreated; and shortly afterwards a group of Bay Area civil libertarians staged a read-in at the Diner, with free copies of *Playboy* supplied by one of Christie Hefner's PR people; and then there was a counter-demonstration by feminist groups, whose members variously opined that "women's health is affected by *Playboy* being in a restaurant," and that the event "had nothing to do with free speech; it had to do with power—power of white men to impose their standards on anyone, no matter how humiliating." If the first law of American corporate life is that dead-wood floats, the corresponding rule of liberation-talk is that hot air expands. As we shall see, America has lately been full of occasions when someone prevents someone else from saying something and then denies it's a free speech issue.

Betty's Diner was comic; other events are much less so. In October 1992 the *Village Voice* sponsored an evening's debate at Cooper Union in New York, on the subject "Can a Liberal be Pro-Life?" The chief speakers were Nat Hentoff and Governor Robert Casey of Pennsylvania, a Democrat who had dissented from the pro-choice plank of the Democratic Convention in New York three months before. Now there were certainly reasons to argue with Casey—as Hentoff later pointed out, there is a glaring inconsistency between his tender regard for fetal rights and his support of the death penalty for adults—but these never got an airing. What happened instead was that a gang of pro-abortion protesters, some wearing buttons that read FUCK FREE SPEECH, took over the hall and prevented any speaker being heard, so that the debate itself was aborted. One of these, a harpy from some obscure left group, later preened herself and her comrades on this victory over free speech in a letter to the *Village Voice*: "When 80 to 100 antiracist and prochoice activists shut down a forum by one of the most powerful racists and sexists in America, as we and others did . . . it is a victory for all progressives." Except, that is, for those progressives who do not believe in the jackboot and the gag, and value debate above Brown Shirt ranting.

Some impulses, one realizes, don't change, they just go underground; there is a direct cable hookup between Cooper Union 1992, Berkeley 1991 and Massachusetts 1670, and it bypasses the Bill of Rights. A couple of years ago, the head of student government at Stanford, young and black, complained that "We don't put as many restrictions on freedom of speech as we should." Precisely the view of Representative Jim Inhofe, Republican of Oklahoma, who at about the same time rose in the House to declare his support of George Bush's flag-protection amendment to the Constitution, with the ringing words "There comes a time when freedom of speech is not in the best interest of this country, and we've reached that point." Palaeo-conservatives and free-speech therapists are both on the same wagon, the only difference being *what* they want to ban.

This whining, denunciatory atmosphere has put quite a load on readers and writers, on how writing is interpreted—and taught.

As our 15th-century forebears were obsessed with the creation of saints and our 19th-century ancestors with the production of heroes, from Christopher Columbus to George Washington, so are we with the recognition, praise and, when necessary, the manufacture of victims, whose one common feature is that they have been denied parity with that Blond

Beast of the sentimental imagination, the heterosexual, middle-class white male.

The range of victims available ten years ago—blacks, Chicanos, Indians, women, homosexuals—has now expanded to include every permutation of the halt, the blind, the lame and the short, or, to put it correctly, the differently abled, the other-visioned and the vertically challenged. Never before in human history were so many acronyms pursuing identity. It's as though all human encounter were one big sore spot, inflamed with opportunities to unwittingly give, and truculently receive, offence. Thirty years ago, one of the epic processes in the assertion of human dignity started unfolding in the United States: the Civil Rights movement. But today, after more than a decade of government that did its best to ignore the issues of race when it was not trying to roll back the gains of the 1960s, the usual American response to inequality is to rename it, in the hope that it will then go away. This, as George Orwell pointed out in *Politics and the English Language,* destroys language without shifting reality one inch. The only safeguard against it, he argued, was to be concrete:

> If you simplify your English, you are freed from the worst follies of orthodoxy. You cannot speak any of the necessary dialects, and when you make a stupid remark its stupidity will be obvious, even to yourself. Political language—and with variations this is true of all political parties, from Conservatives to Anarchists—is designed to make lies sound truthful and murder respectable, and to give an appearance of solidity to pure wind. One cannot change all this in a moment, but one can at least change one's own habits . . .

III

Orwell wrote that in 1946, and it remains true half a century later; indeed, it will always be true. There are certainly worse things in American society than the ongoing vogue for politically correct language, whether of the left or of the right. But there are few things more absurd and, in the end, self-defeating.

We want to create a sort of linguistic Lourdes, where evil and misfortune are dispelled by a dip in the waters of euphemism. Does the cripple rise from his wheelchair, or feel better about being stuck in it, because someone back in the days of the Carter administration decided that, for official purposes, he was "physically challenged"? Does the homosexual suppose others love him more or hate him less because he is called a "gay"—that term revived from 18th-century English criminal slang, which implied prostitution and living on one's wits? The net gain is that thugs who used to go faggot-bashing now go gay-bashing.

Or take "homophobic," a favorite scatter-word of PC abuse. Today, out of twenty people who use it, scarcely one knows what it means. "Homophobia" is a clinical term for a pathological disorder. It means an obsession with homosexuality, caused by the heavily suppressed fear that one may be homosexual oneself. Today it can be, and is, indiscriminately applied to anyone who shows the slightest reserve about this or that same-sexer, or disputes (however mildly) any claims of special entitlement (however extreme) made for them as a group or class. In the 80s one heard American writers accused of "anti-Semitism" if they were Gentiles, or "self-hatred" if they were Jews, because they didn't toe the extremist political line of the Likud party in Israel and its lobbyists in Washington. In stress, angry people who don't have enough language (or whose language is merely the servant of an agenda) reach for the most emotive word they can find: "racist" being today's quintessential example, a word which, like "fascist," raises so many levels of indistinct denunciation that it has lost whatever stable meaning it once had. You can be a "racist" for having crackpot theories of superiority based on the lack of melanin in human skin; or for saying the simple truth that the Rev. Al Sharpton hoaxed New York with the entirely concocted abuse of the black teenager Tawana Brawley by imaginary white goons; or for having doubts about the efficacy of welfare; or, in some minds, merely by virtue of being white.

Just as language grotesquely inflates in attack, so it timidly shrinks in approbation, seeking words that cannot possibly give any offence, however notional. We do not fail, we underachieve. We are not junkies, but substance abusers; not handicapped, but differently abled. And we are mealy-mouthed unto death: a corpse, the *New England Journal of Medicine* urged in 1988, should be referred to as a "nonliving person." By extension, a fat corpse is a differently sized nonliving person.

If these affected contortions actually made people treat one another with more civility and understanding, there might be an argument for them. But they do no such thing. Seventy years ago, in polite white usage, blacks were called "colored people." Then they became "negroes." Then, "blacks." Now, "African-Americans" or "persons of color" again. But for millions of white Americans, from the time of George Wallace to that of David Duke, they stayed niggers, and the shift of names has not altered the facts of racism, any more than the ritual announcement of Five-Year Plans and Great Leaps Forward turned the social disasters of Stalinism and Maoism into triumphs. The notion that you change a situation by finding a newer and nicer word for it emerges from the old American habit of euphemism, circumlocution, and desperate confusion about etiquette, produced by fear that the concrete will give offence. And it is a peculiarly American habit. The call for politically correct language, though some answer it in England, has virtually no resonance in Europe. In France, nobody has thought of renaming the Frankish king Pepin le Bref, *Pepin le Vérticalement Défié*, nor do Velásquez's dwarves show any sign of becoming, for Spanish purposes, *Las gentes pequeñas*. And the chaos that would ensue if academics and bureaucrats decided to overthrow gender-specific terms, in Romance languages where every noun has a gender while, to make things worse, the word for the male genital organ is often feminine and the one for its female counterpart not uncommonly masculine (*la polla/el coño*) hardly bears thinking about.

No shifting of words is going to reduce the amount of bigotry in this or any other society. But it does increase what the military mind so lucidly calls collateral damage in a target-rich environment—namely, the wounding of innocent language. Consider the lumpen-feminist assault on all words that have "man" as a prefix or suffix.

"Man-words" are supposed to be gender-specific and thus insulting to women: "mankind," for instance, implies that females aren't human. So in place of *chairman*, we get the cumbersome *chairperson* or simply *chair*, as though the luckless holder of the office had four cabriole legs and a pierced splat. Recently I was sent the Australian Government's *Style Manual* for official publications, which forbids, among other things, such terms as *sportsmanship, workman, statesmanlike* (whose suggested synonyms are "skilful, tactful"—which may say something about the present lack of Antipodean states-persons, given that in October 1992 our Prime Minister, Paul Keating, robustly denounced the Australian Senate as "unrepresentative swill" and "a bunch of pansies"). Even *craftsmanship* is out; its mellifluous alternative is "skill application." Soon my fellow-countrymen, persuaded by American examples to look for euphemisms where no insults exist, will rewrite *Waltzing Matilda* to begin "Once a jolly swagperson camped by a billabong . . ."

But what is this fuss about "man"? Anyone who knows the history of our language knows that, in Old English and Anglo-Saxon, the suffix *-man* was gender-neutral: it had, and retains, the same meaning as "person" today, referring to all people equally. To denote gender, it had to be qualified: a male was called a *waepman*, a female *wifman*. This gender-free use of *-man* gives us forms like *chairman, fisherman, craftsman*, meaning simply a person of either sex who engages in a de-noted work or profession. The ancient sexist wrong supposed to be enshrined in the word since the time of Beowulf turns out not to exist.[3] Nevertheless it affords ample opportunities for the display of pettifogging PC virtue, as in the following rebuke from one S. Scott Whitlow, an academic in the College of Communications of the University of Kentucky, to Victoria Martin, a student, who passed it along to the *American Spectator*:

Dear Victoria,
    On your recent scholarship application, members of the re-view committee noticed the inappropriate use of the word "chairman" . . . of course, it is especially inappropriate to address

a woman as "chairman" unless she has specifically requested such
a limiting language. . . . Soon you will be entering the corporate
or media sector as you begin your career. There, too, you will
find there are expectations that women not be made invisible
through thoughtless use of language . . . there are a number of
books I would be happy to recommend. Please let me know if
you wish a list.

What is so grating about this tidbit is not just the sloppy
English ("wish a list"), or the bureaucratic vagueness ("entering the corporate or media sector"—this, from someone who
is meant to be teaching *communication!*) or even the condescending use of a stranger's Christian name *de haut en bas*
("Dear Victoria"). It is the anile priggishness of the Puritan
marm, lips pursed, seeking nits to pick.

There are, of course, many new terms and usages that
seemed picky or unnecessary to conservatives when they appeared, but are now indispensable. What letter-writer, grateful for the coinage "Ms," which lets one formally address
women without referring to their marital status, would will-
ingly go back to choosing between "Mrs." and "Miss"? There
is a case to be made for "African-American," though it seems
to have no marked advantages over "black" beyond its length,
a quality of language many Americans mistake for dignity.
Probably the term "Asian-American," vague as it is, is better
than "Oriental," because it is at least decently neutral, without
the cloud of disparaging imagery that still clings to the older
word: "Oriental" suggests a foreignness so extreme that it
cannot be assimilated, and raises the Fu-Manchu phantoms
of 19th-century racist fiction—treacherous cunning, clouds
of opium, glittering slit eyes. "Native American" for American

Indian, or just plain Indian, sounds virtuous—except that it carries with it the absurd implication that whites whose forebears may have been here for three, five or even the whole thirteen generations that have elapsed since 1776 are in some way still interlopers, not "native" to this country. By the time whites get guilty enough to call themselves "European-Americans" it will be time to junk the whole lingo of nervous divisionism; everyone, black, yellow, red and white, can revert to being plain "Americans" again, as well they might.

In any case, words are not deeds and mere nomenclature does not change much. As Barbara Ehrenreich remarked,

> I like being called Ms. I don't want people saying "man" when they mean me, too. I'm willing to make an issue of these things. But I know that even when all women are Ms., we'll still get sixty-five cents for every dollar earned by a man. Minorities by any other name—people of color, or whatever—will still bear a huge burden of poverty, discrimination and racial harassment. Verbal uplift is not the revolution.[4]

Not only is it not the revolution: it has been a godsend to the right. Where would George Will, P. J. O'Rourke, the editors of the *American Spectator* and some of the contributors to the *New Criterion* all be without the inexhaustible flow of PC claptrap from the academic left? Did any nominally radical movement ever supply its foes with such a delicious array of targets for cheap shots?

Satire loves to fasten on manners and modes, which is what PC talk really is: political etiquette, not politics itself. When the waters of PC recede—as they presently will, leaving the predictable scum of dead words on the social beach—it will be, in part, because young people get turned off by all the carping about verbal proprieties on campus. The radical impulses of youth are generous, romantic and instinctive, and are easily chilled by an atmosphere of prim, obsessive correction. The real problem with PC isn't "post-Marxism," but post-Puritanism. Its repressive weight does not fall upon campus conservatives, who are flourishing, delighted that the PC folk give some drunken creep of a student who bellows "nigger" and "dyke" into the campus night the opportunity to posture as a martyr to speech-repression. The students it harms are the kids who would like to find a way of setting forth their dissatisfactions with the way America has gone and is going, but now find they can't speak so freely about them in case they use the wrong word and thus set off flares of complaint and little airbursts of contempt from those on their left. In an academic world where an administrator at the University of California in Santa Cruz could campaign against phrases like "a nip in the air" and "a chink in one's armor," on the grounds that such words have expressed racial disparagement *in other contexts,* anything is possible; how about banning "fruit-tree" as disparaging to homosexuals?[5] And their dilemma is made worse on those campuses, like Stanford, which have created speech codes. These are generally not created by students, but imposed by their elders—Baby Boomer academics, members of a moralizing and sanctimonious generation both left and right. As Nat Hentoff pointed out,[6] these codes, "every one of them so overboard and vague that a student can violate a code without knowing he or she has done so," are not always imposed by student demand, for

At most colleges, it is the administration that sets up the code. Because there have been racist or sexist or homophobic taunts, anonymous notes or graffiti, the administration feels it must *do something*. The cheapest, quickest way to demonstrate that it cares is to appear to suppress racist, sexist, homophobic speech.

Thus a student can be punished under academic law for verbal offences and breaches of etiquette which carry no penalty off-campus, under the real law of the land. This dissociation is rooted in a Utopian fantasy about the nature and role of universities: they are, or should be, Arcadias. But in practice it may impede the student's progress from protected childhood to capable adulthood, which is not an Arcadian state. As one (black, female) community college administrator from Colorado, Gwen Thomas, remarked in the course of a panel discussion at Stanford,[7]

As for providing a non-intimidating educational environment, our young people have to learn to grow up on college campuses. We have to teach them how to deal with adversarial situations. They have to learn how to survive offensive speech they find wounding and hurtful.

IV

The American right has had a ball with Political Correctness. Yet its glee is hollow, and there is something distasteful about its caperings, its pretence to represent "real" language. One would rather swim than get in the same dinghy as the PC folk. But neither would one wish to don blazer and topsiders on the gin-palace with its twin 400-horse Buckleys, its Buchanan squawkbox, its Falwell & Robertson compass, its

Quayle depthfinder and its broken-down bilgepump, that now sits listing in the Potomac as its crew bickers over who "really" lost the 1992 election.

Why? Because the right is as corroded by defunct ideology as the academic left. Propaganda-talk, euphemism and evasion are so much a part of American usage today that they cross all party lines and ideological divides. The art of not answering the question, of cloaking unpleasant realities in abstraction or sugar is so perfectly endemic to Washington by now that we expect nothing else—the main practical difference being that presidents, congressmen, generals and CEOs hire others to write the stuff. The loss of reality by euphemism and lies was twenty times worse and more influential in the utterances of the last two Presidents and their aides than among *bien-pensant* academics, although you didn't find any complaints about that in *Commentary* or the *New Criterion*. Just as managerial lingo gave us "equity retreat" for the 1987 stock market crash and "corporate rightsizing" for firing large numbers of workers, so the Gulf War taught us that bombing a place flat was "servicing a target" or "visiting a site," that bombing it again to make quite sure that not even a snake or a thornbush survived was "revisiting a site." Touchiness about animals and fish has also given us such mincing euphemisms as "harvest" for kill, presumably as in Fenimore Cooper's novel *The Deer-harvester*. Their object is to suggest that hunting is really gathering: canning companies like to put out flackery about "harvesting" tuna, implying that their far-seeing executives had sown the seeds of the albacore and yellowfin and were now merely picking them when ripe.

Gazing on the fall of Communism, conservative columnists wrote about a "unipolar world"—an exquisitely silly piece of late imperial thinking, if you don't happen to be American—and George Bush announced that America now presided over "The New World Order." This uplifting phrase meant nothing. Bush was lucky that the Berlin Wall fell and that the Soviet monolith, its underpinnings rotted beyond repair during the Brezhnev years, collapsed during his Presidency. Sensibly, he did not intervene, and left the liberation of Eastern Europe to the Europeans and Russians themselves.

But at present there is no "New World Order."

Instead, we have an intractable New World Disorder, laced with Arms Business as Usual, as all the nationalist passions and religious hatreds that had been frozen under the Soviet imperial icecap since 1945—some, inside Russia, since 1917—emerge, refreshed by their siesta, impotently watched by the rest of Europe and by the few Americans who can bestir themselves to look up Sarajevo in an atlas, and start killing.

The right has its own form of PC—Patriotic Correctness, if you like—equally designed to veil unwelcome truths. It, too, has a vested interest in keeping America divided, a strategy that bodes worse for the country's polity than anything the weak, constricted American left can be blamed for.

Polarization is addictive. It is the crack of politics—a short intense rush that the system craves again and again, until it begins to collapse. The exacerbated division between "right" and "left" in America comes from reality-loss. It no longer fits the way that most voters respond to politics or envisage their own needs. In the 60s, the New Left tried to label every conservative a fascist. In the 80s, the New Right called every liberal a socialist—and the name stuck. In their unconstrained hostility to everything that descended from the New Deal,

the Reaganites managed to conflate all government interven-
tion in economic life (except the military budget) with creep-
ing Marxism. Then, when real Marxism collapsed at the end
of the 1980s, its death was made out to be a crushing setback
for American liberalism. There was, for a time, a grim humor
in the sight of conservative columnists and editors singing
"Glory, glory, the Soviet Union has fallen apart because of
the far-sighted actions of Ronald Reagan," without noticing
that the USA was coming unstuck for the same reason.

All this was sleight-of-hand. In the last fifteen years American conservatives have had a complete, almost unopposed
success in labeling as left-wing ordinary agendas and desires
that, in a saner polity, would be seen as ideologically neutral—
an extension of rights implied in the Constitution. "I favor
'anti-political politics,' " remarked Václav Havel, shortly after
becoming president of Czechoslovakia. "That is, politics not
as the technology of power and manipulation of cybernetic
rule over humans, or as the art of the useful, but politics as
practical morality, as service to the truth, as essentially human
and humanly measured care for our fellow humans. It is . . .
an approach which, in this world, is extremely impractical and
difficult to apply . . ." In America today, Havel the intelligent
liberal would be as unelectable as Jefferson the elitist slave-
owner. For the idea of "humanly measured care" for the legitimate interests of others is dissolving in a frenzied search for
scapegoats; hysteria over feminism, gay rights and abortion
has filled the discourse of politics with a rancor that has few
parallels in other Western democracies.

The vast majority of American homosexuals are not in
militant groups like Act Up or Queer Nation; they rightly
despise Cardinal O'Connor's views on condoms—as plenty

of us straights also do—but they don't disrupt Mass at St. Pat's; they merely wish to live their lives without being persecuted for their sexual nature.

Yet in the 80s, their call for government action on AIDS got nothing from Washington; Reagan did not pronounce that monosyllable in public once, and from Bush they received little but vague wafflings. Now they have become the subjects of a base rhetorical game, vilified by politicians who expect to win by appealing to intrusive prejudice. Thus in 1992, anti-gay fanatics of the Christian right in Colorado, operating under the name of "Colorado for Family Values," managed to persuade their electorate to erase the state's existing civil rights laws for homosexuals. Henceforth, in Colorado, homosexuals have no protection from job or housing discrimination; threats and violence against them have sharply increased; and skiers in Aspen, as they snuggle into their ecologically correct, fake-fur-lined parkas, may reflect that they are contributing to the prosperity of a state which has now placed itself somewhere near the ethical level of Alabama's race politics in the 1950s.

American feminism has a large repressive fringe, self-caricaturing and often abysmally trivial, like the academic thought-police who recently managed to get a reproduction of Goya's *Naked Maja* removed from a classroom at the University of Pennsylvania. It has its Puritan loonies like the writer Andrea Dworkin who regard all sex with men, even with consent, as a politicized form of rape. Does this in any way devalue the immense shared desire of millions of American women to claim the right of equality to men, to be free from sexual harassment in the workplace, to be accorded the reproductive rights to be individuals first and mothers second?

Yet for some American bigots, feminism is actively diabolical; Pat Robertson, a former candidate for the Presidency who may conceivably run for office again, recently attacked a proposed equal-rights amendment to the Iowa state constitution as part of a "feminist agenda . . . a socialist, anti-family political movement that encourages women to leave their husbands, kill their children, practice witchcraft, destroy capitalism and become lesbians."[8]

When political utterance descends to such levels, fanatics enlist in the crusade but sensible people tend to wash their hands of it. There was little point, as the 1992 election amply showed, in trying to build a party platform on "family values" when what people are really worried about is jobs, or in attempting to sell a campaign for less government which so largely consisted of moving the field of state control out of the corporate boardroom and into the cervix. States tend to look absurd to their own citizens when they try to legislate morality in this way, especially in a country where, polls indicate, clergy are held in lower respect than pharmacists. "Reasonable" voters begin to suspect that the talk about moral values may be a cover-up for the lack of practical social policy. But it is political folly for the "reasonable" to assume that the election of Clinton and Gore in any way neutralizes the large gains made by evangelical groups at the local political level in 1992. On school boards, in city councils and state legislatures, indeed in all areas of American political life outside Washington itself, evangelical bigotry is gathering strength and will continue to do so. When the American economy recovers, there may be fewer people voting against Republican fiscal policy and more voting for the moral promises of an evangelized GOP. Intelligent Americans have no grounds for complacency—not unless they want to hear their kids chirping about the Sin of Sodom and parroting the inanities of "creation science" after school a few years from now. The fundamentalists' drive to annul the constitutional separation of Church and State, to spread theocracy on the land, must be resisted by anyone who cares about democracy in America.

In the 80s, one of the features of the electoral scene was a public recoil from formal politics, from the active reasoned exercise of citizenship. This trend is no longer affordable. It came because Americans didn't trust anyone. It was part of the cafard the 80s induced. In effect, the Republican and Democratic parties since 1968 have practiced two forms of conservative policy, one episodically liberal and the other aggressively not. Both are parties of upper-middle-class interests: the last genuinely progressive tax reform proposed by a President, for instance, was put forward by Jimmy Carter in 1977—and it was immediately sunk by the vote of a Democratic Congress. The whole apparatus of influence in Washington is geared to lobbying by big business, not to input from small citizen groups. As E. J. Dione eloquently argued in his recent book *Why Americans Hate Politics,* there is no bloc in Congress or the Senate that truly represents the needs or opinions of people in the enormous central band of American life where workers and the middle class overlap.

In the early 1970s the Democrats began to lose the confidence of this public by committing themselves to "liberation" politics, focusing more and more emblematically on the rights of minorities and the poor. Listening to liberal Democrats talk in the 70s and early 80s, a foreigner might have supposed that America had only two kinds of people whose political fate actually mattered—the very rich and the ones on welfare.

This line was an artifact of ideology, made from ideas of the late 60s. Democrats rejected their more moderate and pragmatic leaders like Henry "Scoop" Jackson and staked their political future on *cultural* liberation. Like the Republicans in 1992, the Democrats under George McGovern in 1972 tried to run a campaign on moral values—and lost.

Working-class Americans distrusted the "limousine liberals" with their fixations on the environment, women's rights, abortion rights, busing and affirmative action. To talk about blue-collar racism was too simple—it was just another way of schematizing real people from above, and the younger, more ideologically liberal Democrats constantly fell into this trap. American workers saw their jobs and their neighborhoods threatened by policies imposed from above.

And so the Republicans could present themselves as the tribunes of the disparaged values and symbols of the ignored middle, the blue-collar voters who believed in America, mistrusted affluent radicals, and hated flag-burners. It was not immediately apparent that the Republicans cared very little for the economic interests of these people. Who could foresee that their fiscal policies in the 1980s would buy a short-term expansion of the American economy at the cost of $4 *trillion* in debt, thus leading to recession, painful unemployment and the seemingly irreversible decay of public infrastructure? At least the GOP seemed to have an economic policy, though it failed. It was nicknamed the trickle-down theory: the rigidly ideological prescription that a free ride for the rich would generate money for the middling and poor. The Democrats had none that they could sell to an electorate. They didn't like talking about nuts and bolts and jobs. Instead, they mainly talked about rights. They were off in what struck many millions of American voters as a Cloud-Cuckoo land where every pornographer could drape himself in the Jeffersonian toga of the First Amendment, and any suggestion that a child might stand more chance of happiness and growth if it was raised by two parents who loved both it and one another could be pooh-poohed by some ideologue on the left, fresh from the beansprout commune in Vermont. Thus, in Dione's words,

> The moralism of the left blinded it to the legitimate sources of middle-class anger. The revolt of the middle class against a growing tax burden was not an expression of selfishness, but a reaction to the difficulties of maintaining a middle-class standard of living. Anger at the rising crime rates was not a covert form of racism but an expression of genuine fear. . . . Impatience with welfare programs was sometimes the result of racial prejudice, but it was just as often a demand that certain basic rules about the value of work be made to apply to all. Those who spoke of "traditional family values" were not necessarily bigots . . .

This was a value-gap you could barrel a truck through, and the Republicans did so, thus splitting off a large and useful voting-bloc of "Reagan Democrats." But this realliance is proving unstable, now that the actual results of the Republicans' push to unconstrained *laissez-faire* are in: the largest deficit, the most crippling load of debt to foreign lenders, and the widest gap between high and middle income ever to afflict America.

Reaganites talked soothingly about the return of traditional American values, moral contracts, and the like. They showed little sense of a moral contract with African-Americans, because the GOP had seen where the votes lay: in the white suburbs, not the black inner cities. Hence the poisonous error of the Reagan and Bush presidencies: their "Southern strategy" of accommodation towards whatever was most racially divisive in America, their reluctance to treat blacks *as Americans*. Whatever unity they proposed was no more than the specious unity of us-against-them. The famed Willie Horton ad, which sank the 1988 Dukakis campaign, was merely the tip of this iceberg of moral failure.

The GOP's "morality" was all about sex and honoring thy father, and it tactfully avoided other commandments, particularly the one against stealing. Thus one of the prototypical figures of the time was Charles Keating, a Cincinnati businessman with the lantern jaw, piercing eyes and strict ethical look of the risen cracker-salesman. Keating co-founded the National Coalition Against Pornography, with the intent of saving the innocent from Satan, and became a major agitator for "traditional moral values" in the Midwest. Only later did it appear why Keating was so interested in preserving American innocence: he cheated thousands of innocent people of hundreds of millions of dollars in his manipulations of Lincoln Savings and Loan, though—unlike most of his fellow swindlers in this racket—he went to jail for it.

Reaganism did more to uncouple American business from its traditional moorings than any political ideology in the country's history. This orgy, which culminated in the Savings and Loan scandal, went unchallenged by the public at first— mainly because the government kept the public in the dark about what was happening. By mutual consent of the two rival parties, the unpalatable truth that taxpayers must now pony up several hundred billion dollars to bail out the S & L system was not announced until just after the 1988 election. But in any case, the numbers were so huge as to be beyond most people's grasp.

The new business heroes, the corporate raiders and junk-bond merchants—Michael Milken, Ivan Boesky, Kohlberg Kravis—exploded the traditional business relationship between investor, employee and customer; the only interests that mattered, in the new atmosphere of leveraged buyout and tear-down, were those of investors and their agents. This wasn't conservatism. It was more like Jacobinism—a wildly abstracted form of fiscal revolution-by-deed, in which every company, whatever its grounding in former practice and principle, was led before the guillotine of credit. As Michael Thomas put it:[9]

> In such conditions time itself breaks up into discrete parts. An enterprise that may have sunk its roots in commerce and community over a century can be disassembled by a takeover artist in a matter of weeks. Continuum means nothing. Relationships mean nothing. The modern financier lives and dies by the transaction. Each day is wholly new, the wheel subject to endless reinvention. There is no need for coherence because there is no advantage to coherence. Action is all . . . Critical judgment is neutered by celebrity, censure collapses in the face of success.

The 80s brought the fulfillment of Kenneth Galbraith's morose aphorism about America's recoil from the memory of New Deal policies. Private opulence, public squalor.

The traditional role of public architecture in a democracy—to remind the citizen that he or she is the reason for the state, and not vice versa—was cut from the cultural script. America seemed to have no great public buildings or works

projects to show for the 80s. Where were the kind of structures that had stirred its social heart and bolstered its civic
confidence from the 1880s to the 1930s—the symbols of
promethean America, the Brooklyn Bridge, the Golden Gate,
the Empire State Building or, for that matter, Huey Long's
Louisiana State House? Nowhere—only a succession of
ticky-tacky post-modernist confections by Philip Johnson and
his favored younger architects, the pediment-quoting Ralph
Laurens of their profession: formica-thin memorials to the
vanity of this or that corporate raider, gilded Trumpery, visual
propaganda for the empire of Donald Duck. Cultural tourists
came to New York to gaze on its past monuments, as they
once came to Rome; but in the present, they saw only discos,
galleries, trends, the brightly roiled surface of fashion. Every
part of America's public exoskeleton was on borrowed time:
rivets popping from the Williamsburg Bridge, concrete spill-
ing from overpasses, city roads worse than Istanbul's, schools
degenerating, squalid airports. Now and then, down in the
senile guts of Manhattan, a water-main would explode, bringing the subways to a halt; or in Chicago the river would find
its way past a weak point in its subterranean tunnels, and a
repair that might have cost $25,000 (if the bureaucracy had
done it in time) suddenly became a flood crisis that knocked
out the power of the whole city center. Such metaphors of
decay were poignant; they made vivid a pervasive sense of
entropy in the midst of shocking disproportions of wealth, a
hollowness at the cultural core, a retreat from public responsibility.

V

Meanwhile the sense of common citizenship dissolved in a welter of issues that enable Americans to take unnegotiable stands on smaller things, now that they can no longer define themselves against the Big Thing of the Cold War. In William Greider's words, "most [American citizens] cannot imagine the possibility of forming a continuing relationship with power—a political system that would enable them to share in the governing processes and trust in its outcomes." The sense of democratic possibility is "shriveled."[10]

The number of enfranchised Americans who voted in Presidential elections dropped steadily from a high of 63 percent in 1960 to just half the electorate—50.1 percent—in 1988. The 1992 elections registered a modest upturn: a sense of urgency over the sick economy, and Ross Perot's careening appeal to people who felt themselves cut off from Politics as Usual, brought 104 million citizens, representing 55 percent of the voting-age population, to the polls. This figure was encouraging, but it hardly represented a sudden return to civic engagement after the last two decades of voter indifference; it only brought the turnout back to its 1972 level.

Such apathy amazes Europeans and, I should add, Australians.

Why do so many of the citizens of the world's oldest democracy not vote when they can, at a time when the struggle for democracy in Europe and throughout the rest of the world has reached its most crucial and inspiring level since 1848? Partly, it's an administrative problem—the disappearance of the old party-machine and ward system, whose last vestige was Chicago under Mayor Daley. Whatever its abuses, it got people street by street, household by household, to the ballot-boxes. Its patronage system did help tie American people, especially blue-collar and lower middle-class ones, to the belief that they as citizens had some role to play in the running of their country from the bottom up, ward by ward. It reinforced the sense of participatory democracy.

Without it, the poor stopped voting because they believed that nobody in Washington did or could represent them. The less the poor vote, the more the party of the rich will benefit. This produced a vicious spiral, and American electoral techniques reshaped themselves to bypass the lower third of the society, except when it could be selectively stirred by threats of joblessness or veiled appeals to working-class racism. One of the great challenges facing the Clinton administration will now be to reinvest participatory democracy with the meanings it has partially lost—to draw all Americans back into the political process. The fact of Clinton's election, by itself, does not guarantee this; but at least there are grounds for hope.

There is much ground to be rewon. By the late 70s the American citizen was becoming a passive spectator at political events handed down in snippets between commercials. American network television is mostly junk designed to produce reality-shortage, and the average American is said to watch seven or eight hours of the stuff a day. No wonder that the act of pulling the lever every four years seemed to mean less, and that fewer people went to the booth to do it. In the first free election after Franco died, nearly 80 percent of Spain's electorate voted. If 80 percent of American voters voted, as they regularly did in the rough old days of stump politics between 1840 and 1910, that would be a populist revolution; it would mean that Americans really appreciated democracy, instead of just sitting around and making patriotic noises whilst urging democracy on other nations who, not uncommonly, value it by voting more than Americans themselves do.

But it was patriotic noise one got from Washington in the 80s. And who can honestly claim not to be fed up with it? The public face of politics dissolved into theater: a banal drama of pumped-up optimism, fireworks and ballets of Elvis look-alikes at the Statue of Liberty, little cosmetic wars in Grenada and Panama to simulate the sweets of victory after the bitter taste of Vietnam. In the 80s, as never before in America, we saw statecraft fuse with image-management. Too many things in this supposedly open republic got done out of sight of the citizens. Or they were presented in terms that mocked public intelligence by their brevity and cartoon-like simplicity. This was known as "Letting Reagan be Reagan," and it accorded perfectly with the dictates of TV. So the very words that described one's grasp of events mutated: one casualty among dozens was "perception," which used to suggest the act of seeing things truthfully, but in the 80s came to mean "notion" and finally "illusion" or "dumb mistake."

Did the Presidential setup of dazzling stage-lights in front of murky waters have anything to do with the early American ideal of open democracy? The protected power of the CIA and the events of Iran-Contra made a mockery of the vision of open governmental disclosure and civic responsibility that had inspired Jefferson and Madison to campaign against John Adams's repressive Sedition Act back in 1798.

The public face of politics, and especially of the Presidency, was radically overhauled to suit a public attention-span abbreviated by TV. The more argument, and the harsher it is, the more people do vote. So one did not argue: one produced sound-bites, memorable icons of a few syllables. One did not appear; one granted photo-opportunities. One did not write one's own speeches; instead one had hacks to produce vivid, cheap oratorical prose whose function was to create Presidential character. In a sense, the President *was* TV—the world's most successful anchorman. Did he forget things? No matter: TV is there to help you forget. Did he lie? Oh well, never mind. Maybe he just forgot. Or he "misspoke himself." The box is the muse of passivity. With somnambulistic efficiency, Reagan educated America down to his level. He left his country a little stupider in 1988 than it had been in 1980, and a lot more tolerant of lies, because his style of image-presentation cut the connective tissue of argument between ideas and hence fostered the defeat of thought itself. When he appeared before the wildly cheering Republican conventioneers in Houston in 1992, he quoted a passage from Lincoln—"You cannot strengthen the weak by weakening the strong"—that hadn't been written by Lincoln. Its author was a Pennsylvanian clergyman named William Boetcker, who penned it some forty-five years after Lincoln's death. But who was counting? For Reagan's fans, the idea that there ought to be, or even might be, some necessary relationship between utterance and source seemed impertinent to the memory of his Presidency.

This was not a frame of Presidential character that Jefferson or Lincoln would have been likely to imagine—or feel the slightest respect for. Retooled for TV as never before, the Presidential image came out of the box and went straight back into it: for the networks adored it, and the press—most of it, anyway—was not far behind. The big media went right along, because those tropes and tricks and abbreviations were their very own, part of a seamless culture of spectacle. Celebrity politics for an age of celebrity journalism. What began with the Kennedys reached its climax with the Reagans—the fixation on the Presidential person as a substitute king, no longer the *primus inter pares,* first among equals, so radically envisaged by the founders of the republic. But where was the citizen? Outside, as audiences are at spectacles.

Bush lacked Reagan's consoling histrionic power, and to his misfortune the bills accumulated by Reaganite economics began to fall due during his Presidency. In August 1992, the Republican party found itself badly trailing in the polls, without a plausible economic policy, unable to cope with America's vast and growing deficit. It had little of substance to promise a middle-to-working-class electorate that was worried sick about its jobs and its modest investments in the face of a yawning recession. Still, the GOP had to stage a party convention in Houston that would reverse the success of the Democratic Convention a few weeks earlier in New York. The Republicans were in much the same pickle with the voting public as the Conservative party under John Major had been at the 1992 elections in Great Britain. They resorted to the same strategy of division, going for the jugular of fear and distrust, though with a peculiarly American twist which revived the specters of right-wing intolerance in the 1920s and 1950s—and in precisely the same language.

Clinton and Gore had appropriated the lingo of Recovery and group therapy for their campaign pitch; they had gone in soft, dramatizing "concern" and "healing." In a moment of particularly toe-crinkling sentimentality, Gore had related how his son was run over by a car, how he had gazed into the boy's eyes as he hovered between life and death, and how that, fellow Democrats and alienated citizens out there, was like looking at America today. As the oratorical shades of Demosthenes and Burke had once been discerned behind the speeches of Churchill, so those of Oprah Winfrey and Robert Bly could be seen above the Democrats' podium in Madison Square Garden.

But the mild queasiness induced by this imagery was nothing to the rhetorical gross-out of the Republican Convention.

In Houston, the "big tent" under whose ample canvas all kinds and degrees of conservative thought were supposed to gather became the site of a revival meeting. The strategy was to go for deep reflexes with trigger-words, to appeal to prejudice rather than reason or self-interest. The GOP's platform left nothing in the middle ground; it was raw anxious bigotry, aimed to separate America into "us" and "them." The key to this was not economic policy, of course; nor was it even international policy, though much was made of Bush's illusory victory over Saddam Hussein, and there were the usual claims that the fall of Communism in Russia, Germany, Czechoslovakia, Hungary, Poland and the Baltic had far less to do with the Russians, Germans, Czechs, Hungarians, Poles and Balts themselves than with the actions of George Bush in the White House.

No, the key was moral; it was "family values." This phrase was a coercive cliché before the GOP Convention opened, and by its third day not even the happiest-married person could hear it without wincing. For if the American right had a monopoly on the virtues of the nuclear family, and knew how to fix them in the time of their supposed decay, why did they come adrift during the last twelve uninterrupted years of Republican power? Better not to ask. There was a real

America, a true core America, which had these "family values." Its paladins were George Bush, Dan Quayle, and the religious right. There was a false America, a perverted and cynical America, which did not. Its visible agents were liberals and their friends: homosexuals, feminists, tree-huggers and spotted-owl freaks, Hollywood and "the media," meaning all journalists, print or electronic, except the one the Vice-President or his aides happened to be giving an interview to at the time. ("I don't mean objective responsible media people like you, Bill, but . . .") Some of these folk did not actually exist in the real world: thus Quayle was able to attack a fictional character, Murphy Brown, for having a baby out of wedlock—rather as some disaffected Elizabethan might have cited Doll Tearsheet, the whore in *Henry IV,* as evidence of moral decay at Hampton Court. Real and unreal, such people constituted a "cultural elite" whose mission was to discredit and trash the "family values" of the real America.

To announce the battle Patrick Buchanan, Bush's recent conservative opponent, was called to the podium. He gave a speech so harsh and divisive that it might not have been out of place in the Reichstag in 1932. It contained nothing that Buchanan had not said a hundred times before: the same putrid stew of gay-bashing, thinly veiled racial prejudice, black Irish paranoia and authoritarian populism continued to bubble beneath the commonfellow surface. Two decades before, John Mitchell, as crooked an Attorney-General as America ever had, called this "positive polarization; and Pat Buchanan, then a young speechwriter for Richard Nixon, sent his President a memo on the uses of divide-and-conquer politics: "If we tear the country in half, we can pick up the bigger half." This was entirely in the spirit of Buchanan's boyhood hero,

Joe McCarthy. To divide a polity you must have scapegoats and hate-objects—human caricatures that dramatize the difference between Them and Us. If some part of a political strategy can turn, as it now does, on the act of inflaming prejudice against homosexuals and denying them certain rights as a class or group, then so be it; and so much the worse for the people whom in the past Buchanan had called promoters of "Satanism and suicide," "perverted," "destructive," a "pederast proletariat"—all those lisping armies of the night out there, sneaking up on *your children,* not just on consenting adults! God's little ally, the AIDS virus, was "divine retribution" against such people, just as, to the fundamentalist preacher of the 1920s, the spirochete and the gonococcus had been launched against the rake and the seducer by an offended God. Nothing had changed.

VI

But then, why should it? Apart from the vastly more efficient means of dissemination, the databases and faxes and instant-polling devices and other tools of info-blitz, there is little new about either these effusions of patriotic and pious bigotry, or the codewords that announce them. Nor was it altogether surprising that the American electorate, wiser than pundits often suppose, should have rejected them and voted, instead, on realer issues—mainly, the depressed economy.

Such movements, such forms of rhetoric appear in America whenever deep change impends.

In the 1890s the Populists sought to counter the confused

identity of an America in radical flux from immigration with their virulent anti-Semitism, their nativism and their religious bigotry. The hate-objects were recent immigrants, Jews and Irish Catholics, rather than "liberals" as such. Precisely because America is a country of immigrants, it is the older arrivals, now rooted, who always resist the irruption of the new stranger. This distress was found at all levels of American culture at the century's end, high and low, just as it is today. The Irish had Tammany Hall, the aggrieved Jews opposed it; in 1902 a Jewish funeral procession, passing through an Irish industrial district of New York, was pelted with iron machine-parts and some two hundred Jewish mourners were clubbed down by Irish cops.[11] Ninety years later similar scenes of bigotry against "the unassimilated stranger," this time involving Jews and blacks, would be played out in Brooklyn.

In the 1920s, once again, due to the increase of big industry, the rapid growth of cities and a new influx of millions of European Catholics and Jews, traditional Protestants closed ranks against the "alien; the WASP felt, in Lipset and Raab's words, that he "was losing control of the society which his father had dominated and which he had expected to inherit as his birthright."[12] This defensive impulse was particularly strong among Christian fundamentalists in the "heartland," who felt menaced by the growing dominance of "city culture" and the way in which relativism and science were loosening America's grasp on biblically revealed truth. The "monkey trial," in which J. T. Scopes, a Tennessee teacher, was arraigned for expounding Darwin's theory of evolution to his pupils, was only the most visible sign of a nationwide reaction against pluralism. The idea that many moral and intellectual positions could coexist within the frame of democracy repelled these American monists, who desired only one orthodoxy, one revealed truth. To them, in the 1920s as in the 1990s, disagreement was illegitimate and the "market of ideas" invalid. The extreme of this was summed up in the apocryphal remark attributed to a Baptist preacher, that a man needed only one book on his shelf: for if an idea was in the Bible you needn't look any further for it, and if it wasn't it would be wrong anyway. The monist ("one-truth") line runs exactly counter to Thomas Jefferson's wise prescription: "If there be any among us who would wish to dissolve this Union or change its republican form, let them stand undisturbed as monuments of the safety in which error of opinion may be tolerated where reason is left free to combat it."

Today, America is not "heading back" to the 1920s or to the McCarthy years of the 1950s. Like fungal spores in the soil, these repressive tendencies are always there, always latent, and capable of fruiting overnight given the right conditions. Their appearance is cyclical, and their tenacity deflates one's optimism about moral progress in 20th-century America. But the objects on which they fix can change, since this kind of ultra-conservative reaction lives by personifying social fears of the Other; Joseph McCarthy's effects on American social morale had little to do with the number of Communists he actually found in government, but everything to do with the ways he found to break the American polity by projecting a half-human, half-demonic shape of dread on the amorphous anxieties of his time. There were Soviet agents in America, though it now seems fairly certain that Alger Hiss was not one; parts of the media became "soft on Communism" through the pro-Soviet bias of some writers and editors; spies did steal atom secrets; and traitors were at work. Many liberals in America turned a blind eye to the atrocious realities of government under Stalin and Mao, just as their counterparts did in France and Italy, and would continue to do through the 1960s and even into the 1970s. But none of this quite explains the intensity of the McCarthyite witch hunt, its apocalyptic grip on the American imagination.

McCarthy's success lay in unlocking the vast reserves of American monism, the long-hoarded nativist intolerance of difference, and allowing that to play on the specifically ideological issue of Communism-versus-liberal democracy just at the moment that America went to war with a Communist regime, North Korea. McCarthyism was less a political movement than a Children's Crusade, an irrational quasi-religious event. It owed both its initial success and its eventual collapse to the diffuseness of its targets, their lack of bodies and names. McCarthyism, opportunistic by nature, had a blurred focus. Which *Americans* embodied the enemy ideas? "The closest McCarthy came to personifying a group as that enemy in America," Lipset and Raab pointed out, "was his attack on the elite."[13] The elite—meaning the well-off, well-educated, brightest-and-best of eastern WASPdom—"have been selling the nation out," McCarthy declared, through their "traitorous actions."

Shifting blame to an elite, or declaring your enemies to be one, is one of the oldest tools in the demagogic kit. Elites are snobbish, out of touch with the people, arrogant, secretive and plain un-American. Best of all, their members need not be named. Shortly after Vice-President Quayle fluttered the dovecotes with his speech about the "cultural elite" in 1992, a TV interviewer asked him to name some of its members. He refused to, coyly adding that "we all know who they are."

With Communism gone, the politics of division needs other "outsider" and "deviant" groups to batten on, such as homosexuals. It also needs people or symbols to idealize. Hence the efforts to claim the flag for "us," the American right alone; to fetishize it to the point where it becomes not just a national symbol, but a kind of eucharist, so sacrosanct that it must have a constitutional amendment (no less!) to protect it from misuse. Hence, too, the bizarre politics and imagery of the new Sacrificed Body of American conservatism, the fetus.

When the person laying siege to the abortion clinic declares himself to be "Pro-Life," we may be sure that he's not worrying about the life of the scared pregnant teenager; what is at stake is not so much the survival of the fetus, as the issue of how much male control over the bodies of women this society will grant. For without the right to choose abortion over pregnancy, the idea of equal opportunity for women fails: the involuntary mechanism of ovary and womb will always hamper their pursuit of degrees, appointments, jobs and free time. The growing conservative obsession with legislating against "choice," of trying to hustle a grave moral decision which is inherently personal into the domain of public law, can only prove, in the end, a disaster for conservative interests. It will do to them what strict Roman Catholic doctrine on contraception has already done to the Catholic Church.

The image of the fetus has established a strange presence in American popular culture, one which has no parallels elsewhere in the West. It made a bizarre appearance at the closing ceremonies of the 1992 Olympic Games in Barcelona, capering on the stage of the Montjuic stadium, eight feet high or so, apparently made of foam plastic, moved by a dancer inside it, flashing a fixed white grin as inane as a 70s Smiley-face sticker. This, the announcer proclaimed, was "Whatizit," the official emblem of the 1996 Atlanta Olympics. Tiny limbs, goggly eyes, an oversize body, a vestigial tail on which the five Olympic rings were coyly threaded like quoits on a stick. What Walt Disney did to the duck, some team of American designers had done to the fetus. The fetish of the religious right is now an Olympic mascot. No wonder the Catalans were perplexed.

Does this portend a wave of Fetus Chic for '96? Unlikely, but there are bound to be millions of Whatizit souvenirs, as there were millions of Cobis in Barcelona—fetus lapel-pins, fetuses promoting Coke, inflatable fetuses, cuddly fetuses covered in synthetic plush, little fetal paperweights. Close your eyes and see a new hotel by Michael Graves, its pediment supported by fetal caryatids, all in the form of Whatizit. This prospect suggests how deep the image of the fetus has sunk into the weird stew of American media-consciousness, with a third of the country obsessing about the Unborn and another third vaporing about its Inner Child.

Did the designers sit down with some committee for Atlanta '96 and decide to make a Games logo in the form of a fetus? It seems improbable. Fetuses do not suggest sport. They are, on the whole, as unathletic as little pashas. Supine in their amniotic fluid, they do not practice the butterfly or the Australian crawl; they do not even begin to kick—let alone jump, run for extended periods, cycle or show signs of proficiency with a target pistol—until they are almost babies. No, Whatizit is not a conscious image; he is a phantom of the *Zeitgeist,* a case of overspill, or precipitation, from fetus-overload in popular culture. Semiologists, if one wanted to get fancy about it, would call him a floating signifier. He would not exist without those demonstrators brandishing their plastic babies at the abortion clinics on the six o'clock news; without the two Pats of the fanatic right, Robertson and Buchanan, ranting about innocence. Only in America could a fetus pass so quickly from the symbol of a "cultural war" to the logo for a sports event. Whatizit is a cute reminder of an issue that is not at all cute.

This is why Whatizit is going to get very intrusive as the Games approach, and gratuitously bothersome. He already bothers me, and I have only seen him once so far—but then, being an ex-Catholic, I am readily irked by such matters. In the comparatively simple and absolutist frame of Catholic upbringing in Irish Australia forty years ago, there wasn't the enormous ambiguity about abortion that America has today; it was simply assumed that abortion was murder, unthinkable, *tout court,* no argument about it. Where the stress lay was on contraception, and on the "right to life" of the spermatozoon. Crammed with unruly testosterone, two hundred of us boys would sit in the boarding-school chapel listening to a priest expound the moral theology of this. God, one learned, had put the sex-drive in us for two reasons. The first was to ensure the propagation of the species. The second was to give plea-sure, thus holding legitimate marriages together. It was wrong to short-circuit God's first purpose in order to get to the second, especially if you weren't married. Primary pur-poses, secondary purposes: this arid quibble, designed by celibate theologians, has helped to drive countless Catholics out of the Church. Masturbation might not make you blind, or cause a single black hair to sprout unstoppably from the palm of your hand—the Jesuits, on the whole, were above such coarse Protestant fright-tactics. But every sperm was sacred, being a potential human being: more like a microscopic tadpole right now, but capable of turning into a person once it hit an egg, and therefore to be honored and preserved along with its millions of siblings. Every time you wanked, it was a slaughter of future Catholics so small that a hundred of them could dance, or at least wiggle, on the head of a pin. The real trouble with masturbation was that it represented an inversion of the cosmic order—and contraception, even worse. The notion that some small part of the cosmic order hung on our teenage willies was a heavy load for us young soldiers in St. Ignatius' army of Christ. In some of us, including Private Hughes, it induced the kind of suffocating guilt that led to skepticism: if God was so busy counting sperm, and so apparently unconcerned with preventing the world's famines, epidemics and slaughters, was He worth worshipping? Was He there at all? No answer from the altar.

Something of this fetishism continues to haunt the abortion debate—to the point where Cardinal O'Connor, in a speech to the national convention of the Knights of Columbus in New York in August 1992, felt moved to propose that a "tomb of the unborn child" should be erected in every Roman Catholic diocese in America. This, not the Olympics, would be the right spot for Whatizit. We are to value the three-month fetus or even the embryo, that insentient piece of highly organized tissue attached to the uterine wall, above the interests of the mother not because of what it *is*, but for what it *may become*. The primary purpose of women is to be mothers and ensure the continuation of the species; their secondary purpose is to be self-sufficient people, with rights over whatever their bodies contain; if the two conflict, the second must lose. This is the iron law of abstraction. No decent person pretends that abortion does not present a grave moral choice, but the whole point is that this choice must be made by the mother, not denied her by the state. Nobody—except those who believe, on no evidence at all, that an immortal soul really is implanted in the embryo at the moment of conception, thus endowing it with complete humanity—can say at what point an embryo turns into a human being.

The innocence of fetuses is not in doubt. But it is irrelevant: lettuces are innocent too. Fetuses do not sin because they cannot sin. They cannot sin because, at least as far as anyone can detect, they have no free will and are not presented with the occasions of sin. The womb is short of temptation. It is like the Garden of Eden, before the snake. Presumably this is why the anti-abortionists, with their PC jargon of innocence and potential, prefer the unborn to the born: in the act of being born, we fall into an imperfect world, whereas the fetus, like the distinctly unborn-looking Star Child surrounded by a caul of light in Kubrick's *2001,* is an emissary from a perfect one—the uterine state, the Womb with a View, of which all our expensive comforts from sofas to heated swimming-pools are only metaphors. This may be one reason why the opposition to abortion grows more extreme as the material circumstances of America grow worse.

Just twenty years ago, when Philip Roth published *Our Gang,* his wonderfully corrosive lampoon against Richard Nixon, he imagined the President setting out to run for office on the votes of the "embryos and fetuses of this country"— who will gratefully remember

> just who it was that struggled in their behalf, while others were addressing themselves to the more popular and fashionable is-

sues of the day. I think they will remember who it was that
devoted himself, in the midst of a war abroad and a racial crisis
at home, to making this country a fit place for the unborn to
dwell in pride.

There was hardly a book-critic in America who didn't take
Roth to task for going over the top, exceeding the permissible
limits of satire, and the rest. (*Time* magazine, among others,
refused to review it at all.) Canvasing fetal votes! Who ever
heard of such a thing! *Our Gang* was the only satire written
by a modern American fit to be compared to Swift's *A Modest
Proposal*. But unlike the Dean's vision of a starving Ireland
nourished on the flesh of its surplus babies ("I have been
assured by a very knowing *American* . . . that a young healthy
Child well Nursed is at a year Old a most delicious, nourish-
ing, and wholesome Food"), Roth's has, in a general way,
come true. There are moments in America when reality out-
strips the powers of satire, and the "abortion issue"—or so
one felt, while watching one orator after another blowing
steam at the 1992 National Republican Convention in Houston about the sacred rights of the unborn and the need for a
Constitutional amendment to outlaw abortion, even in the
case of pregnancies caused by rape or incest—has turned out
to be one of these.

VII

By the 80s the American left was a spent taper in national
politics. Its only vestiges of power were cultural. It went back

into the monastery—that is, to academe—and also extruded into the artworld.

The main target of McCarthyism was the heritage of New Deal liberalism from the 30s. The main target of the conservative push of the 80s, as Paul Berman pointed out, was "the heritage of democratic openness and social reform that dates from the radical sixties"—including the part of that heritage, wacky or sensible, that surfaced on campus.[14]

The middle-to-highbrow form of the assault is the ongoing frenzy over "radical," leftist influences within academe, meant to warn Americans that although the ideology of totalitarianism has collapsed in Europe and Russia, it survives in China, Cuba—and American universities. By this reading, a "new McCarthyism," this time of the left, has taken over the campus and is bringing free thought to a stop. The culture, warns Hilton Kramer in *The New Criterion,* is "in deep and terrible trouble." The academy has internalized the Barbarians who once assailed it and "this barbarian element—so hostile to the fundamental tenets of our civilization . . . now commands an immense following in our mainstream institutions. It has already radically transformed the teaching of the arts and humanities in our colleges and universities." Not everyone who thinks so is a neo-conservative, either—in 1991 no less eminent a historian than Eugene Genovese, writing in *The New Republic,* affirmed that "As one who saw his professors fired during the McCarthy era, and who had to fight, as a pro-Communist Marxist, for his own right to teach, I fear that our conservative colleagues are today facing a new McCarthyism in some ways more effective and vicious than the old."

Other (mostly younger) academics fervently deny the Mc-

Carthyism charge, calling it an overheated metaphor. And indeed there is little sign of a repetition of what the senator from Wisconsin and his cronies actually did to academe in the 50s, usually through pressure on administrators and faculties who regarded themselves as liberals: the firings of tenured profs in mid-career, the inquisitions by the House Un-American Activities Committee on the content of libraries and courses, the campus loyalty oaths, the whole sordid atmosphere of persecution, betrayal and paranoia. The number of conservative academics fired by the lefty thought police, by contrast, is zero. There has been heckling and stupidity. There have been baseless accusations of racism, like those flung at the historian Stephan Thernstrom at Harvard, who took the view—scandalous to PC-mongers—that in studying the history of American slavery, one should attentively read the historical evidence on both sides, including the record of how slaveowners and pro-slavery writers defended the practice. Certainly there is no shortage on campus of the zealots, authoritarians and scramblers who view PC as a shrewd career move or as a vent for their own frustrations.

Nor is it a fantasy of the right that almost anyone teaching the humanities in an American university today is going (at the very least) to be badgered by PC attitudes and will need a robust independence of mind to resist them. The process is akin to the old American religious one of shunning and shaming. It will also help determine which teachers get hired and which don't. And it is given strength by the sheer size of American academe, the inflation of its numbers, the sense that the academic audience is practically a mass audience anyway so that nobody need think of readers outside its self-referential and all-too-often conformist boundaries. No question, the academy has gotten too fond of the tags and labels that substitute an easy moralism for thought and judgment—racist, sexist, homophobic, progressive, reactionary. The uniforms in its current war of mice and frogs may look novel, but the war itself is not so very new—or so one is reminded by Auden's "Under Which Lyre":

> But Zeus' inscrutable decree
> Permits the will-to-disagree
>   To be pandemic,
> Ordains that vaudeville shall preach
> And every commencement speech
>   Be a polemic.
>
> Let Ares doze, that other war
> Is instantly declared once more
>   'Twixt those that follow
> Precocious Hermes all the way
> And those who without qualms obey
>   Pompous Apollo.
>
> Brutal like all Olympic games,
> Though fought with smiles and Christian names
>   And less dramatic,
> This dialectic strife between
> The civil gods is just as mean,
>   And more fanatic.

However, one may well be skeptical of the standard neoconservative charges that American academe has been taken over by the militant left—by a cabal of "Visigoths in tweed," in the words of Dinesh D'Souza, author of the 1991 bestseller *Illiberal Education: The Politics of Race and Sex on Campus*. A picturesque phrase—but also one that makes one wonder about D'Souza's grasp of the Western values whose survival worries him. If he knew about Visigoths he would also know that in the 6th century they did wonders to consolidate the battered remnants of Roman order in Spain, that their legal code is justly regarded as one of the true monuments of Western jurisprudence, and that on instituting Christianity as their state religion they embarked on a large and costly program of church-building. They could hardly have done better if they were led by William Bennett and Cardinal O'Connor. In truth, there has scarcely been a time since the Russian Revolution when the American right was *not* fretting about the number of "tenured radicals" (in Roger Kimball's phrase) installed at American universities, and how different things are now from the better and less ideological past. It is common to read about the academies' fall into "politicization" compared, say, with the 1950s. But then one finds the distinguished philosopher Sidney Hook, in *Heresy, Yes. Conspiracy, No* (1953), advocating a bar against Communists teaching in American colleges, and claiming that a thousand Reds were already teaching, just in New York schools:

> Even if each teacher, on a conservative estimate, taught only a hundred students in the course of a year, this would mean that every year one hundred thousand students in New York City alone would be subject to educationally pernicious indoctrination. Of these . . . hundreds would have been influenced by their teachers to join Communist youth organizations from which the Communist movement draws its most fanatical followers.

'Tis ever thus, one is tempted to assume. If the Marxists are, indeed, on the point of taking over the academy in the 1990s, they seem to be rather secretive about it—though that, of course, may be due to their Machiavellian habits of dissimulation. Recently, when the Higher Education Research Institute at UCLA did a survey of 35,000 professors at 392 schools, it found that only 4.9 percent of them called themselves "far left" while 17.8 percent (more than three times as many) put down "conservative." All the rest described themselves as "liberal" or "moderate." Even at Berkeley, the *locus classicus* of student radicalism in the 1960s and 70s, only one person out of thirty in the sociology department now calls herself a Marxist.

Such figures should be treated with a degree of caution: not all American colleges are as tolerant of teachers with left-wing views as the elite ones of the Ivy League or the California state system, and an extreme political timidity prevails on community-college campuses. There are still good reasons why an academic, pressed for answers in a survey, might make himself out to be more centrist than he is. Nevertheless, within limits, the results of that survey are probably indicative.

When one hears the often-repeated conservative charge that the modern American campus is "politicized," it is worth remembering that it always was. The idea that, before the 1960s, academe was a kind of ideal state of objective study, free from contamination by political interests and political bias, is a myth: it's just that in the postwar years the political pressures went the other way, and entailed using the campus as a source of information for the FBI and a recruiting-ground for the CIA.

If someone agrees with us on the aims and uses of culture, we think him objective; if not, we accuse him of politicizing the debate. In fact, political agendas are everywhere and the American conservatives' ritual claim that their own cultural or scholarly positions are apolitical is patently untrue. There are leftists of various stripes in the lit and humanities departments—but why should there not be? Universities must expose their students to debate, and genuine debate *should* include the left, the right and the center, particularly in times as conservative as these. The proper objection to left-wing argument at American universities is not that it exists, for it ought to exist and prosper freely—it's that so much of it is opaque, filled with jargon and devoted to marginal issues. But what of the conservative figures who, in the main, occupy the major funded chairs at American universities and run the big campus institutes of economics, management and government, from the Harvard Business School on down? Major American universities are big businesses, disposing of immense investments in stock and real estate, plugged into government by countless advisory pipelines. It is inevitable that their paths of preferment run on conservative tracks. They always have. It is absurd to pretend this is "apolitical."

Much of the traditional teaching in American schools, though not necessarily the machine of thought-bending its critics now claim it was, has been rather less "disinterested" than it seems. A case in point is the basic Western Civ course itself. As the historians Carol Gruber and William Summerscales have shown, the Western Civ classes—a quick once-over in the "cultural values" and "background" of European civilization—actually entered the American curriculum when, and because, America got into World War I.[15] The American government wanted its college-trained doughboys to know what they were fighting for, and a "War Issues" or propaganda course was devised for this purpose. Its aim was to produce what an editorial in *The History Teacher's Magazine* at the time felicitously called "thinking bayonets." It would set American youth straight about Teutonic frightfulness. After the Armistice, this course was developed by Columbia College into "Contemporary Civilization," the prototype of modern Western Civ classes—this time, with a view to producing students who would be made, in the words of one Columbia dean, "safe for democracy" by inoculating them against the new threat of Bolsheviks, "the destructive element in our society."

The truly intractable difficulty of American higher education today is not its ideological content, but the state of preparedness of its students. This problem lies far back, in the high schools, where "disadvantaged" students—mainly black—receive a basic education that is shockingly inferior to white ones. Bad education inflicted years before college level has assured, as a survey of the National Assessment of Educational Progress found in the late 80s, that among 21-to-25-year-olds, only 60 percent of whites, 40 percent of Hispanics and 25 percent of blacks could "locate information in a news article or an almanac"; only 44 percent of whites, 20 percent of Hispanics and 8 percent of blacks could correctly figure the change due to them after paying a restaurant bill; and only 25 percent of whites, 7 percent of Hispanics and 3 percent of blacks could grasp the content of a printed bus schedule. No university can solve that tragic situation and only the most radical improvement of secondary schooling can combat it. It is not the students' fault. During the 1980s, black American students on their way to college, though falling below the white average on the SAT, actually raised their national average of combined verbal and math SAT scores by 49 points— by a bitter irony, just at the time that the Reagan administration was cutting the amount of federal college scholarship money available to the poor.

Universities, in seeking a quick fix to the anguish of unequal education, may compound the problem. Is the answer
to drop entrance requirements as a form of "affirmative action"? In the late 80s, the University of California's Berkeley
campus decided that the proportions of new students admit-
ted—black, Hispanic, Asian and white—should roughly fol-
low the demographic distribution of these groups in the larger
society of northern California.

The problem was that, of the high school graduates seeking a place at Berkeley, 30 percent of the Asians—Chinese-
and Japanese-Americans—qualified, as against 15 percent of
the whites, 6 percent of the Chicanos, and only 4 percent of
the blacks. There was no mystery as to why: the Asian kids
worked hard and came, on the whole, from close-knit families
which supported them and kept their noses to the grindstone.
So Berkeley simply changed its admission standards. Henceforth blacks needed only to score 4800 points out of 8000
to get in, but the threshold for Chinese- and Japanese-
Americans was pegged at 7000. Naturally, when word of this
got out into the Asian community, there was outrage and
protest. Nevertheless the idea keeps lurking in the American
higher-education system that black or other minority students
can somehow be "empowered" and brought onto the "level
playing-field," by rigging entrance standards. But all a university can reasonably hope to do, in this disputed area, is to
help the *intelligent* disadvantaged over hurdles more easily
cleared by the *intelligent* advantaged. A more equitable policy,
as Dinesh D'Souza and others have argued, would be to link
preferential college admission to a student's poverty, not to
his or her race. Universities are institutions of higher learning,
not (at least, not primarily) of social therapy. Do they have
the right to lower their admission standards and teaching

levels so that the disadvantaged can catch up, at the expense of the educational rights of abler students? If you believe that colleges ought to be training-grounds for elites, however broad-based access to them ought to be, then the answer has to be no. But the main current of opinion, among teachers who came of age in the 60s or later, is passionately, almost reflexively, against elitism. "The prevailing ideology," wrote the educator Daniel J. Singal,[16] "holds that it is much better to give up the prospect of excellence than to take the chance of injuring any student's self-esteem. Instead of trying to spur children on to set high standards for themselves, teachers invest their energies in making sure that slow learners do not come to think of themselves as failures . . . one often senses a virtual prejudice against bright students."

If the causes of poor performance among black students, compared with Asian or white ones, lie too far back in the school system to be corrected at the university door, then lowering the qualifications for black (or any other) students is, in the words of the historian Eugene Genovese, "a charade . . . If, as should be obvious, some people, black or white, begin with less cultural advantage, less preparation, and less talent than others, 'equality of opportunity' can only result in the perpetuation of the initial levels of inequality."[17] What sustains these attempts at social therapy, in Genovese's view, is "the radical egalitarian conviction that everyone is fit for, and has a right to, a college education. . . . We have transformed our colleges from places of higher learning into places for the technical training of poorly prepared young men and women who need a degree to get a job in a college-crazy society." If America did not place such unreal emphasis on college degrees, this problem might not vanish, but it might at least deflate. A college degree is not necessary for most jobs that people do in the world, whereas literacy, numeracy and basic skills at interpreting information are absolutely so. (Or such, I should perhaps add, is my own experience, being a college dropout without any degrees.) The main effect of American degree-fetishism has been to make skilled pragmatic work seem second-rate. It has demeaned the objects of Walt Whitman's great litany in "A Song for Occupations":

> Strange and hard that paradox true I give,
> Objects gross and the unseen soul are one.
> House-building, measuring, sawing the boards,
> Blacksmithing, glass-blowing, nail-making, coopering,
>   tin-roofing, shingle-dressing,
> Ship-joining, dock-building, fish-curing, flagging of
>   sidewalks by flaggers,
> The pump, the pile-driver, the great derrick, the coal-
>   kiln and brick-kiln,
> Coal-mines and all that is down there, the lamps in the
>   darkness, echoes, songs, what meditations, what
>   vast native thoughts . . .

Moreover, Singal warns, not enough thought has been given to a growing crisis at the other end of the social, racial and educational spectrum: the better-off students, mostly educated in suburban schools, who since the mid-1970s "have been entering college so badly prepared that they have performed far below potential, often to the point of functional disability." In 1970 new students came into leading colleges (Columbia, Swarthmore, the University of Chicago) with average verbal SATs ranging from 670 to 695 out of a possible

800. By the mid-1980s these averages had dropped to a range of 620 to 640. Exactly the same pattern, with a few areas of exemption (mainly the better Southern universities, where test scores *rose* after full desegregation), has held true across the U.S. Once there, the education they receive (when their teachers are not struggling to bring them up to levels of reading and comprehension they should have reached in high school) is downscaled to their reduced ability to read texts, sift information and analyze ideas. Thus it becomes an impoverished coda to the intensive learning students were once offered, and to the expectations that were made of them; geared to the students' limited experience of life and ideas as though this were some kind of educational absolute (whereas, of course, it is the thing that real education seeks to challenge and expand), mushy with superficial social-studies courses that inculcate only buzzwords and are designed, as far as possible, to avoid hard questions of historical context, it is short on analysis and critical scrutiny but long on attitude and feeling. The full results of this emasculation will appear in the 90s, and the political-correctness flurry—which is all about feelings, and more common, it seems, among teachers than among the students themselves—is merely one of their premonitory symptoms. For when the 1960s' animus against elitism entered American education, it brought in its train an enormous and cynical tolerance of student ignorance, rationalized as a regard for "personal expression" and "self-esteem." Rather than "stress" the kids by asking them to read too much or think too closely, which might cause their fragile personalities to implode on contact with college-level demands, schools reduced their reading assignments, thus automatically reducing their command of language. Untrained in

logical analysis, ill-equipped to develop and construct formal arguments about issues, unused to mining texts for deposits of factual material, the students fell back to the only position they could truly call their own: what they *felt* about things. When feelings and attitudes are the main referents of argument, to attack any position is automatically to insult its holder, or even to assail his or her perceived "rights"; every *argumentum* becomes *ad hominem,* approaching the condition of harassment, if not quite rape. "I feel very threatened by your rejection of my views on [check one] phallocentricity/ the Mother Goddess/the Treaty of Vienna/ Young's Modulus of Elasticity." Cycle this subjectivization of discourse through two or three generations of students turning into teachers, with the sixties' dioxins accumulating more each time, and you have the entropic background to our culture of complaint.

VIII

In cultural matters the old division of right and left has come to look more like two Puritan sects, one plaintively conservative, the other posing as revolutionary but using academic complaint as a way of evading engagement in the real world. Sect A borrows the techniques of Republican attack politics to show that if Sect B has its way, the study of Plato, Titian and Milton will be replaced by indocrination programs in the works of obscure Third World authors and Californian Chicano muralists, and the pillars of the West will forthwith collapse. Meanwhile Sect B is so stuck in the complaint mode that it can't mount a satisfactory defense, since it has burnt most of its bridges to the culture at large (and denies, in its more narcissistic moments, that the general intelligent reader still exists—though the worse problem is the shortage of general intelligent *writers*). With certain outstanding exceptions like Edward Saïd, Simon Schama, David Hackett Fischer or Robert Darnton, relatively few of the people who are actually writing first-rate history, biography or cultural criticism in America have professorial tenure, though many writers are attached to universities as decorative hermits or trophies in those therapeutic diversions known as Creative Writing courses. ("I am astonished," wrote the boxing Dadaist Arthur Cravan in a philippic against art schools, back in 1914, "that some crook has not had the idea of opening a writing school." Now we know better.) But on the whole, most contact between academe and the general intelligent reader seems to have withered, because overspecialization and the *déformations professionnelles* of academic careerism are killing it off.

Within the lit and humanities departments of the modern American university the angle of specialization—of topics, of ways of thinking, and above all of language—has become so narrow, so constipated by the minutiae of theory, so pinched by the pressure to find previously unworked thesis subjects, that it can't extend into a broader frame. Most of its discourse has no hope of reaching a lay audience. Fine, says the defense: who expects the work of a research scientist at MIT to be read, or even faintly comprehended, by laymen? People are working out there on the edge of mathematics and quantum physics in areas so rarefied that no more than thirty other specialists, world-wide, can understand their papers; and so what? Isn't it the job of universities to support "useless" knowledge, meaning areas of scientific research that have no apparent bearing on the way most people live and are incomprehensible to all but a tiny handful, in the justifiable belief that they may in time become very "relevant" indeed? Science has a thousand blind alleys for every path that becomes a public highway, and research must explore them all—or perish.

All true; but the trouble with applying this to the humanities is that the appreciation of art and literature has no scientific basis whatever; one is dealing in the unquantifiable coin of feeling, intuition and (from time to time) moral judgment, and there is no objective "truth" to which criticism can lay "scientific" claim. The critic Louis Menand points out that the binding institution of American academic lit-crit, the Modern Language Association (MLA), was founded in 1883 by philologists, "scholars whose work *was* scientific and could therefore be evaluated 'objectively.'" Not until 1950 would the MLA add the word "criticism" to its charter; and it only did so because criticism presented itself as increasingly grounded in theory, and hence as a contribution to *knowledge,* not just to the sum of opinion. Obsession with theory, combined with lack of writing talent, creates the awful prose of academic lit-crit. Nobody wants to return to the old ways of harrumphing, "humanistic" belles-lettrism that held sway before the "New Critics" took over forty years ago, but the present state of university writing about the arts today is somewhere between a sleeping-pill and a scandal.

To justify their existence when the model of American higher education was scientific, lit departments had to survive by claiming that they were on the cutting edge of new techniques. Hence the "foregrounding," as jargon has it, of dialects that relate to nothing outside the academy; hence, too, the disconnection between academic criticism and the far clearer writing on kindred subjects in the non-academic press. As Menand argues,

> . . . most of the academic world is a vast sea of conformity, and every time a new wave of theory and methodology rolls through, all the fish try to swim in its direction. Twenty years ago every academic critic of literature was talking about the self, its autonomy and its terrible isolation. Today not a single respectable academic would be caught dead anywhere near the word, for the "self" is now the "subject" and the subject, everyone heartily agrees, is a contingent construction . . . what ought to be most distressing to everyone is the utter predictability of the great majority of the academic criticism that gets published.[18]

The status of research and publication is high, and that of actual teaching disproportionately low. More and more, students are required to do research hackwork for the teacher's upcoming paper. American universities preserve, as though in amber, the medieval apprenticeship system. In part, this has been forced on them by the expansion of academe itself. When there are so many students that the professors can't teach them all, and funds are limited, the answer is to use "teaching assistants," paid at sweatshop rates; when the professor sees his or her academic duty as lying more in publishing than in teaching, he can call on a pool of "research assistants"—his own students—to do his work for him. Some see this as good training for the dissenting and questioning mind. Others, with at least as much reason, see in it a form of indenture, leading to conformity and opportunism.

When the old New Left students of 60s academe re-entered the university as teachers, they saw the exhilarated hopes of their youth deflate after 1968, collapse under the backlash of the 70s, and become mere archaeology by 1980. None of the beautiful promises came true.

Their response to this trauma was to shift away from classical Marxism, with its emphasis on economic and class struggle in the real world, and embrace the more diffuse and paranoia-driven theories of the Frankfurt school—Theodor Adorno, Herbert Marcuse.

For these theorists, all human life was ruled by repressive mechanisms embedded, not in manifest politics, but in language, education, entertainment—the whole structure of social communication.

To this was joined the belief of French poststructuralism, exemplified by Michel Foucault and Jacques Derrida, that the "subject"—the thinking, single agent, the "I" of every sentence—was an illusion: all you had left was language, not mentality: frustration with pervasive systems of repressive undecidability written everywhere in the surrounding culture, but no means of overcoming it. Once there were writers, but now there is only what Foucault derisively called "the author function." The intellectual, under these conditions, is thought to be as helpless against power and control as a salmon in a polluted stream, the only difference being that we, unlike the fish, *know* the water is poisoned.

Thus, by the theory, we are not in control of our own history and never can be. We hold it true that truth is unknowable; we must suspect all utterances, except the axiom that all utterances are suspect. It would be difficult to find a worse—or more authoritarian—dead end than this. John Diggins, in

The Rise and Fall of the American Left, puts it in a nutshell: "Today the intellectual's challenge is not the Enlightenment one of furthering knowledge to advance freedom: the challenge now is to spread suspicion. The influence French post-structuralism enjoys in American academic life . . . answers a deep need, if only the need to rationalize failure." The intellectual who imagines he or she can challenge the status quo by arguing the uselessness of language starts with not one, but three strikes against him, and this is why poststructuralism, though it has filled the seminar rooms for the last decade and given us a mound of largely unreadable cultural criticism along with some preachy neo-conceptual art, has had so little lasting effect on the way people in general write, think, or act. It is mostly an enclave of abstract complaint.

Outside its perimeter, real life, real language and real communication go on. In the late 80s, while American academics were emptily theorizing that language and the thinking subject were dead, the longing for freedom and humanistic culture was demolishing the very pillars of European tyranny. Of course, if the Chinese students had read their Foucault they would have known that repression is inscribed in all language, their own included, and so they could have saved themselves the trouble of facing the tanks in Tiananmen Square. But did Václav Havel and his fellow playwrights, intellectuals and poets free Czechoslovakia by quoting Derrida or Lyotard on the inscrutability of texts? Assuredly not: they did it by placing their faith in the transforming power of thought—by putting their shoulders to the immense wheel of the word. The world changes more deeply, widely, thrillingly than at any moment since 1917, perhaps since 1848, and the American academic left keeps fretting about how phallocentricity is inscribed in Dickens's portrayal of Little Nell.

The writer who drops in on this world is bound to feel like Gulliver visiting the Royal Academy of Lagado, with its solemn "projectors" laboring to extract sunbeams from cucumbers, build houses from the roof down and restore the nutritive power of human shit, all convinced of the value of their work. I am also reminded of Australia, the home of lost biological causes: just as the pouched macropods and egg-laying mammals, the kangaroos and wallabies and echidnas and platypi, flourished undisturbed on their drifting fragment of the mother-continent Gondwana eons after they were extinct everywhere else on the globe, so the last Derrideans and Lyotardians and Baudrillardians are still hopping and snuffling around in American academe, years after their intellectual mentors ceased to interest the French themselves. And these are the people who complain about cultural colonialism!

In the late 80s the editor of the Presses Universitaires de France, Nicos Poulantzas, was struggling to complete an expansive series of books on Marxism and contemporary life that had been started in the 70s: Marx-and-cooking, Marx-and-sport, Marx-and-sex, Marx and anything you cared to mention. But it was unfinishable: long ago, Poulantzas had run out of Marx-fixated French writers. "Our only hope is America," he confided gloomily to a colleague, shortly before he committed suicide.

The fact that Marxist influence so endures in the American academic left—to the point where you can still find an Althusserian or two—is a proof of the power of nostalgia. There is and always will be reason for the young to study Marx—starting with the fact that the 20th century is incomprehensible without a grasp of the immense impact his ideas, and others' interpretations of his ideas, have had on world politics.

Nevertheless, Marxism is dead; that part of history is over. Its carcass will continue to make sounds and smells, as fluids drain and pockets of gas expand; Europeans who were once Communists will continue to be reborn as ultra-nationalists, like the genocidal former apparatchik, President Slobodan Milosevic of Serbia. Many who satisfied their taste for bureaucratic power within the imperial structure of Communism will continue to slake it at the new fountains of local nationalism.

Such people, however unworthy of respect, are at least more realistic than intellectuals who sigh for the lost promise of Marx and Lenin. For the fact is that Marxism lost its main bet at the outset. It wagered its entire claim to historical inevitability on the idea that humankind would divide along the lines of class, not nationality. In this it was wrong. Because the bonds of nationhood were so much stronger than those of class, the Revolution could only be exported in three forms: as direct conquest by Moscow, as in eastern Europe; by the reinvention of ancient, xenophobic, authoritarian structures with a "Marxist" veneer, as in Mao's China; and as a handy form of rhetoric which gave "internationalist" legitimacy to nationalist chieftains and *caudillos,* as in Ceacescu's Romania, Castro's Cuba or any number of ephemeral African regimes. But the basic promise of Marxism, an *internationale* of workers joined as a transnational force by common interests, turned out to be a complete chimera. Nationalism survives. Half a century after Hitler's death, neo-Nazi gangs march, hold hate-rock concerts and burn sleeping Turkish migrants in Germany; even Mussolini's granddaughter is in Italian politics. Whereas forty years after Stalin's death, there isn't a true-red

Marxist believer in power, or even *near* power, anywhere in Europe.

Marxism has no promise for America. Since 1917, it has failed after three-quarters of a century of tests in every society where it was applied. It has produced nothing but misery, tyranny and mediocrity. The fact that it often replaced other systems which were also tyrannous, mediocre and miserable does not mitigate its failure. The historian learns never to say "never," but all the same it is highly improbable that large numbers of people, in the imaginable future, will submit themselves to the yoke of a political ideology that assumes that mankind is capable of objectively discerning, judging and controlling everything that exists in terms of a "rational," "scientific" program, a single model propagated by central planning. Marxism set itself against nationalism, spread by adapting to it, and in the end was laid low by it.

Here lies the extraordinary irony of the present American debate over "multiculturalism." The academic left professes to see in it the seeds of radical promise: Marxism has passed through the fires of its own dissolution and is reborn as a "hero with a thousand faces"—multiculturalism. To entertain this fiction is to act as if the fundamental conflict between Marxist-Leninism and national diversity had never existed; as though there was some residue of truth in the now violently rejected claims that Marxism increased a nation's awareness of its own being. Moreover, what's left of the Left would like to endow ordinary internal differences within a society—of gender, race and sexual pattern—with the inflated character of nationhood, as though they not only embodied cultural differences but actually constituted whole "cultures" in their own right. "Queer Nation," indeed, where the mere fact of one's carnal appetites is imagined to provide sufficient basis for one's political identity. At the same time, American conservatives are apt to take this futile attempt to draft multiculturalism into post-Marxist system-saving as though it represented some kind of reality. There is no Marx left to fight; so forth we go in knightly array against the vague and hydra-headed Multi. Thus both sides are trapped by mutual obsession, in an otherwise empty side-trench of an extinct Cold War.

How could any genuine multiculturalist—anyone who cares about differences of culture, aspiration, and history between societies or groups—give allegiance to a doctrine that sought, in the name of "liberation," to imprison all human difference within the same internationalist, pseudo-scientific model? Moreover, *Pace* the hard-liners, you do not have to be an ideologue to spot human oppression and injustice, and to want to do something about it; long before *The Communist Manifesto,* men and women burned with indignation when they saw the strong depriving the weak of hope, and they will keep wanting to redress the injustices the rich inflict on the poor long after the last Marxist regime collapses.

Yet the effort to save some notionally "pure" essence of Marx's ideas from their results in the real world still goes on, despondently, in America—because America, unlike Russia or China or Cuba, has never had a Marxist government, or anything resembling one, so that the millenarian hopes and fantasies of Marxism never had a chance to be tested. Thus American radicals have always been able to disport themselves in the ideal promises of Marxism, without having to live with the wretchedness of their fulfillment. Just as Christianity would end if the Messiah were to return, so it is only possible to keep some kind of Marxist faith after the collapse of

European Communism by redefining oneself as a "post-Marxist" and focusing on language rather than deeds.

Hence, in the universities, what matters is the politics of culture, not the politics of the distribution of wealth and of real events in the social sphere, like poverty, drug addiction and the rise of crime. The academic left is much more interested in race and gender than in class. And it is *very* much more interested in theorizing about gender and race than actually reporting on them. This enables its savants to feel they are on the cutting edge of social change, without doing legwork outside of academe; the "traditional left" has been left far behind, stuck with all that unglamorous and twice-told stuff about the workers. It is better to rummage around in pop culture, showing how oppressive structures are "inscribed" in some of its forms and "questioned" by others—a process inseparable, of course, from the protean energies of capitalism, seeking to re-invent its oppressive self every day through popular culture in order to find new and better ways of turning us into docile consumers. Inflation and devaluation are built into this search for small objects on which theory and metatheory can build their large, freeform incrustations. What matters is the *amount* of "knowledge-production" and not its quality. Thus, in the words of the Chicago professor of English and education, Gerald Graff,[19]

> narrow canons of proof, evidence, logical consistency and clarity of expression have to go. To insist on them imposes a drag upon progress. Indeed, to apply strict canons of objectivity and evidence in academic publishing today would be comparable to the American economy's returning to the gold standard; the effect would be the immediate collapse of the system.

This attitude has spilled over into all areas of cultural criticism, and is *de rigueur* in most of them.

Madonna is a particular focus for such riffs. She has become the prime pinup of American academe, robed in peekaboo theory, now filmy, now opaque. As Daniel Harris pointed out in *The Nation*,[20] she "has been drafted into the staggeringly implausible role of spokeswoman of the values and professional interests of university instructors." There is a Lacanian Madonna, a Baudrillardian Madonna, a Freudian Madonna, a Foucaultian Madonna—rather as, in Mediterranean Catholic cults, one may pray to the Madonna of Loreto, of Fatima, or of Lourdes. If you are a Marxist-feminist scholar like Melanie Morton, you can show that her melodies "prevent what we would call in narrative terms an ideological closure. There is no recapitulation which fixes power and establishes (or reestablishes) any element as dominant."

Thus the blonde bombshell explodes the established order of power. She undermines "capitalist constructions" and "rejects core bourgeois epistemes"—a proposition that would certainly be news to my own employers at Time Warner, who recently paid Madonna $60,000,000 for the rights to her work. Some rejection. The truth is less radical: some academics want a little slice of the action of spectacle provided by mass culture. Dazzled by its shine and yackety-yack, they are more groupies than rebels. The sequence is predictable. Ice-T or Sister Souljah do their raps about killing whitey, and call themselves "revolutionaries." A CEO at Time Warner, which distributed Ice-T's exhortations to cop-killing, then defends the corporation's right to produce such stuff in terms plangently reminiscent of Milton's *Areopagitica*. After these pieties, scholars weigh in with learned papers on the revolutionary promise of sixteen-year-olds in the 'hood. Up come the conservatives, wringing their hands in the manner of the late Allan Bloom over rap, rock-'n'-roll, and the unearned Dionysiac ecstasies of mass multi-culti. Somewhere along the line the obvious fact that rap and hip-hop are not the agents of a desired or feared apocalypse, that they are just another entertainment fashion, gets lost. And it is lost because one side needs the other, so that each can inflate its agenda into a chiliastic battle for the soul of America. Radical academic and cultural conservative are now locked in a full-blown, mutually sustaining *folie à deux,* and the only person each dislikes more than the other is the one who tells both to lighten up. Such is the latest mutation of America's Puritan heritage.

If the American left is to revitalize itself, it will have to relearn plain English, return to the actual and resistant world, reclaim not only the Enlightenment principles but the language of Tom Paine and Orwell for itself—and it will never do that with its present encumbrance of theory. All that preserves the illusion of radicalness in academic poststructuralism and neo-Marxism is the conservative opposition. The right needs a left: if the battlements of Western culture were not under continuous siege, what would happen to their defenders? All the cash flowing to neo-con watchdog causes from the copious coffers of the Scaife family and the Olin Corporation would dry up. (The choir of conservatives denouncing "well-subsidized left academics" as bludgers, whilst taking their own subsidies from various right-wing foundations, is truly one of the wonders of American intellectual life.) As American conservatism confronts the death of Marxist ideology, its nurturing enemy, one is irresistibly reminded of the question posed by Constantine Cavafy eighty years ago:

What does this sudden uneasiness mean,
and this confusion? (How grave their faces have become!)
Why are the streets and squares rapidly emptying,
and why is everyone going back home, so lost in thought?
    Because it is night and the barbarians have not come;
    and some men have arrived from the frontiers
    and they say that barbarians don't exist any longer.
And now what will become of us without barbarians?
    They were a kind of solution.

The favorite all-purpose Barbarians, at present, are called "multiculturalists."

LECTURE 2
Multi-Culti and Its Discontents

*T*HE OBSESSIVE SUBJECT of our sterile confrontation between the two PCs—the politically and the patriotically correct—is clumsily called "multiculturalism." This has become a buzzword with almost as many meanings as there are mouths to utter it.

Much mud has been stirred up by the linkage of multiculturalism with political correctness. This has turned what ought to be a generous recognition of cultural diversity into a worthless symbolic program, clogged with lumpen-radical jargon. Its offshoot is the rhetoric of cultural separatism.

But separatism is not, as some conservatives insist, the inevitable result of multiculturalism. The two are in fact opposites.

Multiculturalism asserts that people with different roots can co-exist, that they can learn to read the image-banks of others, that they can and should look across the frontiers of race, language, gender and age without prejudice or illusion, and learn to think against the background of a hybridized society. It proposes—modestly enough—that some of the most interesting things in history and culture happen at the interface between cultures. It wants to study border situations, not only because they are fascinating in themselves, but because understanding them may bring with it a little hope for the world.

Separatism denies the value, even the possibility, of such a dialogue. It rejects exchange. It is multiculturalism gone sour, fermented by despair and resentment, and (in America, if not in Bosnia-Herzegovina or the Middle East) it seems doomed to fail. To use the cultural consequences of American diversity as a tool for breaking the American polity only breaks the tool itself.

Its six syllables are awkward, this word "multiculturalism," but if it had existed thirty years ago when I was getting ready to leave Australia I would have embraced it at once. The expatriate surrenders some part of his native culture—you can't take it all with you—in exchange for what he will pick up on his travels. To learn other languages, to deal with other customs and creeds from direct experience of them and with a degree of humility: these are self-evidently good, as cultural provincialism is not.

One of the more disagreeable moments of my education was having to stand up and speak extempore in Latin for four minutes, before other schoolboys and our Jesuit teacher, on Horace's famous tag, *Coelum non animam mutant qui trans mare currunt*—"those who cross the sea change the sky above them, but not their souls." I resented this, not only because

my Latin was poor, but because the *idea* struck me as wrong—
the utterance of a self-satisfied Roman, impervious to the rest
of the world. Hegemonic Horace.

But most Australians were on his side. The motto of Sydney University expressed contentment with the colonial bind:
Sidere mens eadem mutato, another version of Horace's imperial thought—"The same mind under changed skies."

Our education would prepare us to be little Englishmen
and Englishwomen, though with nasal accents. We would
not be accepted as such by the English themselves: we were
not up to that. No poem written by an Australian was going
to make its way into the anthologies of English verse—our
national fate was to read those anthologies, never to contribute to them. It seemed natural to us that our head of state,
with constitutional power to depose any democratically
elected Australian prime minister, should be a young English-
woman who lived 14,000 miles away. What native-born Australian could possibly be as worth looking up to as this Queen?
Our Prime Minister, Robert Menzies, last of the true Australian imperialists, said we were "the Queen's men," "British to
the boot-heels." When asked what his dream of felicity would
be on leaving politics, he unhesitatingly replied, "A book-
lined cottage in Kent."

In those days we had a small, 95 percent white, Anglo-
Irish society, in whose public schools you could learn Latin
but not Italian, ancient but not modern Greek. What we
learned of the world in school came through the great tradition (and I use the word without irony) of English letters and
English history. We were taught little Australian history. Of
the world's great religions other than Christianity—Judaism,
Buddhism, Hinduism, Islam—we were as perfectly ignorant

as a row of cats looking at a TV set; or would have been, if
Australia had had television in 1955, which, luckily, it did
not. I didn't meet a Jew until I got to University, and you
can imagine the line the Jesuits took on the Spanish Inquisi-
tion and the policies of Ferdinand and Isabella. I didn't even
know what an *Episcopalian* was. Not until my late teens did I
have a conversation with an Australian Aborigine, and it was
short. There were no Aboriginal students, let alone teachers,
at Sydney University. The original colonists of Australia—
whose ancestors had walked and paddled there, across the
string of islands that lay between "our" continent and Asia,
around 30,000 B.C.—were completely unknown to us city
whites, and their history and culture fell into a box marked
"anthropology," meaning the study of exotics with whom one
had nothing in common, and whose culture had nothing of
value to contribute to ours. Thinking so was our subliminal
way of warding off the suspicion that ours had contributed
nothing but misery and death to theirs.

My father, who was born in 1895, was like every other
Australian of his generation when he spoke of Asia. He saw
it as a threat—not surprisingly, since Australia had been at
war with Japan from 1941 to 1945, and lost many young
men in the Pacific islands, in New Guinea, on the Burma
Road and in hellish concentration camps like Changi. Only
by a hair's breadth and the force of American arms did we
escape being forcibly co-opted into what Tojo called the
Greater East Asian Co-Prosperity Sphere.

Such national experiences, mixed with a long tradition of
Sinophobia—for the racially exclusive White Australia Policy
was a left-wing law, originally designed to keep cheap coolie
labor out of Australia—did not predispose even intelligent

Australians, like my father, towards an appreciation of Zen calligraphy or the finer points of tea. He kept a captured Japanese flag in a cupboard (not on the wall) and sometimes I would take out this rusty square of cotton with the brilliant red circle and the frayed rip in it, which I assumed to be a bullet-hole, and reflect that but for the grace of God it might now be flying over Royal Sydney Golf Club. (The Japanese, at the time, did not play golf.)

Who talks of "Asia" or "Asians" now—even as we utter our vague generalizations about "European" culture? There are only Chinese, Japanese, Indonesians, Cambodians, and within even these national categories lie complexities of identity and heritage that are lost on the distant foreigner. But my father thought even more abstractly than this. He rarely mentioned Asia to me. He called it the Far East, meaning the Near North, and would not have considered going there. Far East of where? East of Eden: that is, east of England, a country in which, by his death, he had spent less than three of his fifty-six years, in between tours of duty flying a Sopwith Camel in France for his King and Empire in World War I. Today, if you asked a twelve-year-old Australian boy what he thought about "the East," he might hesitate: what does the oldie mean? New Zealand is in the east; maybe he means that, or Peru, which is even farther east.

So you might say that my upbringing was monocultural, in fact classically colonial, in the sense that it concentrated on the history, literature and values of Western Europe and, in particular, of England, and not much else. It had very little relationship to the themes of education in Australia today, which place a heavy stress on local history, the culture of minorities, and a compensatory non-Anglocentric approach to all social questions. "Multiculturalism" has been a bureaucratic standard there for the best part of twenty years now, and its effects have been almost entirely good. It reflects a reality we have in common with the even more diverse, but culturally reluctant, USA—which, put in its simplest terms, is that the person on the bus next to you in Sydney is just as likely to be the descendant of a relatively recent arrival, a small trader from Skopelos, a mechanic from Palermo, a cook from Saigon, a lawyer from Hong Kong or a cobbler from some *stetl* in Lithuania as the great-great grandchild of an Englishman or Irishman, transported or free. The length of one's roots, as distinct from their tenacity, is no longer a big deal in my country, whatever passing pangs of regret this may induce in the minority of Australians whose families have been there for most of its (white) history. By the 1970s Australia had ceased to be a "basically British" country anyway, and there was no feasible way of persuading the daughter of a Croatian migrant of the mystic bond she was supposed to feel with Prince Charles or his mother—or of the enduring usefulness, to her education, of the history of the Plantagenets. It is probable that young Australians, away down there in what so many Americans still persist in imagining as a sort of Texas conducted by other means at the bottom of the globe, have a far better picture of the rest of the world—Near North included—than their American equivalents have or are likely to get. They have been given it by education and, of late, by television: the Australian government sponsors not just a few programs but an entire network channel, SBS, broadcasting seven days a week, which presents news, documentaries, film and commentary from all over the world, in twenty languages from Arabic to Tagalog (with English subtitles). One can imagine the howls of outrage about "cultural fragmentation" that would issue from the mandarins of American conservatism if Washington were to even think of spending taxpayers' money on such a scheme in the United States. Yet if SBS's programming has any effect on the Australian polity, it is probably to cement it through mutual tolerance and curiosity rather than to fragment it into zones of cultural self-interest. In Australia, no Utopia but a less truculent immigrant society than this one, intelligent multiculturalism works to everyone's social advantage, and the conservative crisis-talk about creating "a cultural tower of Babel" and so forth is seen as obsolete alarmism of a fairly low order.

II

So was my education in the early 50s deceptive? I am reluctant to think so—but I would be, wouldn't I?

Recently I came across a book by one of my fellow students at Sydney University, who in the 1950s was still a relatively raw émigré, a "New Australian: a Hungarian Jew named Andrew Riemer, who arrived from Budapest with his parents in 1946, suffered the humiliations of Australian exile (which included being shunted into a class for intellectually retarded children because his English was bad), and now teaches English literature at Sydney University. *Inside, Outside* (1992) is a tender and perceptive memoir of what it was like to grow up between the Anglo-Oz and the migrant cultures of our raw, awkward, imaginatively impoverished country, and at one point the author puts his finger on one of the reasons why the early Anglocentric education we all received was not, after all, without its value. Riemer was a city boy, and in the early 50s the hard beauty and peculiar delicacy of the Australian bush did not enter into Australian suburban experience; the transformations of sensibility caused by the Australian environmental movement, which are commonplace there now, had hardly even begun. "Nothing in our environment suggested that nature could be a source of wonder or consolation, let alone transcendence." His teachers and mentors failed him by not even suggesting that Australian nature could be culturally inspiring: "for them it was merely desert, the awful emptiness of an empty world." The gap this left was filled by English poetry, especially nature-poetry:

> True, the experience was vicarious, perhaps gimcrack . . . but Tennyson's words represented for us an essential experience which we could not approach in any other manner. His poetry, and that of Wordsworth, Keats and Shelley . . . provided an escape from and a consolation for the ugliness and meanness of the world in which we were forced to live. Neither the physical world we inhabited, nor any of the poetry produced by it, could provide such escape and consolation. . . . The literature of England conducted us into the world of the romantic imagination which served one of the essential needs of adolescence. It also catered generously for others: a heroic or noble past in which we could participate, and ethical structures to provide models for fantasies, if not for actual life.[1]

"These," Riemer adds with some understatement, "are contentious issues to raise in the current climate of cultural nationalism." Yet they certainly strike a chord in me, although (as an expatriate) I feel Riemer goes too far when he adds, speaking of the present, that "Nothing in the contemporary educational and cultural climate [of Australia] caters for those powerful longings—romantic, idealistic, seeking for beauty which the individual finds hard to recognize or to define—that our membership of the British world provided for us through books, through a version of history, and through models of behaviour which these structures recommended to us." This is no longer true in young Australians' experience of their own landscape, which tends to be enthusiastic and informed—though not without its ironies. (CONSERVE AUSTRALIAN NATURE, ran a graffito in Sydney recently, and beneath it another hand had added PICKLE A POSSUM.) And no doubt the "version of history and models of behavior" that Australians of my age and Riemer's found in British imperial iconography can be supplanted from Australian sources—the problem being to embrace those sources, which means leaping clear of the double-bind of colonial history, a task which engages many Australian writers besides myself. A necessary prelude to this will be the cutting of the last political cords that tie Australian government to the British Crown and the establishment of an Australian Republic. The point is, however, that one should indulge in neither the Cultural Cringe (the belief that nothing in Australian culture is worthwhile until it has been certified overseas) nor its defensively brash successor, the Cultural Strut, in which one marches up and down to the tune of "Waltzing Matilda" pretending that nothing made outside Australia is "relevant" to Australians. The right attitude is neither cringe nor strut, but a natural and relaxed uprightness of carriage. Perhaps this also applies to the many advocates of cultural group-separatism (black, Latino, Indian, feminist, gay, what you will) whose din fills the spaces of America with an often shaky rhetoric of "pride" and "entitlement."

When I was young I found that reading the 18th- and 19th-century English poets did not make Australia invisible. Quite the contrary. It pointed me towards reading those Australian poets whose project was to describe Australian nature, history and social experience in images that made sense to Australians—writers like Kenneth Slessor (in *Five Bells*), Robert Fitzgerald (in *The Wind at Your Door*), Judith Wright or, twenty years down the line, Les Murray. It is a truism, but true nevertheless, that a writer should be open to all literature; that its national or tribal forms and sentiments should not be experienced as mutually exclusive. The idea that the ex-colonial must reject the art of the ex-colonist in the interests of *political* change is absurdly limiting. And its absurdity remains true no matter what form of "colonization" is meant—economic, sexual, racial. You can learn from Picasso without being a phallocrat, from Rubens without becoming a Hapsburg courtier, from Kipling without turning into an imperialist. The particular feeds on the general, and vogue-words like "Anglocentrism" or "Eurocentrism" are wretchedly crude devices for describing the complex, eclectic processes by which the individual imagination and a common culture form one another, reciprocally, with much feedback and many cancellations, through the medium of language. Where I come from, "Euro" is also the Aboriginal name for a large kangaroo. In an important essay published in 1977, and thus predating most of America's present multiculturalist debate, Les Murray described how the influence of Aboriginal culture and its song-cycles entered his work, even as it was "implanting the

Aboriginal concept of the sacredness of the land and of one's native region in the minds of many Australians." The main conduit for this was T. G. H. Strehlow's monumental compilation *Songs of Central Australia,* which appeared in 1970. Such a perception of myth deeply grounded in landscape could not help but present itself, even as it built (in the work of a white poet of Scots descent) upon English poetic traditions, as an alternative to the colonial perception of Australia as an empty field of otherness, sterile and dull when compared with the "fullness" of Europe. Already, in the 1970s, there was a political guilt-current in (white) Australian culture hostile to such perfusions, accusing their (white) makers of exploitation, paternalism and so forth. But, as Murray argued,[2]

> It will be a tragedy if the normal processes of artistic borrowing and influence, by which any culture makes part of its contribution to the conversation of mankind, are frozen in the Aboriginal case by what are really the maneuverings of a battle for political power within the white society of our country, or by tactical use of Third World rhetoric. . . . Artistic borrowing . . . leaves the lender no poorer, and draws attention to his riches, which can only be depleted by neglect and his loss of confidence in them; these cause them to be lost. Borrowing is an act of respect which may restore his respect for his goods, and help to preserve them. And he is at all times free to draw on them himself.

So despite the present mania for disparaging Eurocentrism, I know I was lucky to get the schooling I did. It was broad, "elitist" in its emphasis on performance, and rigorous—its sheer workload, the number of books we were expected to read and absorb, would strike a modern American pupil as cruel. It left no "time for smelling the roses," in that favored phrase of American liberal educators (which usually translates as watching TV). This did us no harm at all. We either passed, or we failed and repeated the year, and the report cards went to our parents, whose feelings were not spared. We were made to learn things by heart and read them aloud, with the result that some of them stuck. (I have never agreed with the conventional belief that rote learning of texts destroys a pupil's "creativity"; actually, it enriches it by filling the wells of memory.) We bitched about the discipline sometimes, but were on the whole proud to be in the Jesuit cavalry and not the Christian Brothers infantry. Some of us were snobs, and some embryo fanatics, but that's adolescence. In sum, this Eurocentrist, single-religion core curriculum gave us a point from which we could later branch out.

The critic of Eurocentrism would say that it implanted a permanent bias. Maybe, but you can't see other cultures well until, through knowing your own, you reach a point where inclusiveness means something. Otherwise you're left with mere indecisive mush.

If I now react against the idea of centralized, imperial culture, if I am more interested in difference than supposed mainstreams today—and if I was not, I would hardly have written a longish book about Barcelona and Catalan nationalism—the impulse probably began because Father Wallace made me read Byron on Hellenism when I was fifteen. If I can handle a few Romance languages that I never heard spoken in Australia, it's partly because Father Fraser taught me Catullus and Ovid, not shirking their erotic and skeptical side. If I can sight-read one of the great Baroque churches of Mexico, like Santo Domingo in Oaxaca, and reflect on what makes it both like and so very unlike others in Spain or Italy, it's ultimately because I learned a common ground of iconography as a boy, in that school chapel full of ugly plaster saints. And though the Jesuits' preoccupation with the classics didn't leave any room for Arabic history, it certainly prepared me to change my mind about Islam when I later discovered how little of the written heritage of Greece and Rome would have survived without Arabic scholarship.

So I would say that my own environment, though highly monocultural, was not monolithic: it gave me the tools to react against it, which I did by leaving, living elsewhere, and getting interested in the hybrid, the impure, the sense of eclectic mixture that lies at the heart of so much of 20th-century creation. Culture and history are full of borders but they are all to some degree permeable. And America is one of their classic sites: the place filled with diversity, unsettled histories, images impinging on one another and spawning unexpected shapes. Pilgrims land on a rock in 1620, totally unaware that Spaniards had begun to build Santa Fe ten years before; and why should one chain of history be given marked precedence over the other in school textbooks? The history of Spaniards in America is not for Hispanics alone. The history of blacks is not for blacks alone. No minority or group can be written out of American history, because the very nature of its narrative enfolds them all.

This polyphony of voices, this constant eddying of claims to identity, is one of the things that makes America America. It is, I repeat, why the foreigner is grateful to be here. Hence when I hear Pat Buchanan, another nice Irish Catholic boy, ranting about the likely effect of importing "a million Zulus to North Carolina," and how we must not surrender the single, apostolic, Christian and European essence of American culture to the unspecified multiculturalist hordes . . . well, the gut sinks and the hackles rise.

Nothing could be less like the tiny homogeneous Australia of my childhood than this gigantic, riven, hybridizing, multiracial republic, which each year receives somewhere between a half and two-thirds of the world's emigration, legal or illegal. By the year 2000, less than 60 percent of the people entering the American workforce will be native-born whites. To put the argument for multiculturalism in merely practical terms of self-interest: Though elites are never going to go away, since the need to create them is written in our biological fabric—whether we choose to kid ourselves about this or not—the *composition* of those elites is not necessarily static. The future of American ones, in a globalized economy without a Cold War, will lie with people who can think and act with informed grace across ethnic, cultural, linguistic lines. And the first step in becoming such a person lies in acknowledging that we are not one big world family, or ever likely to be: that the differences between races, nations, cultures and their various histories are at least as profound and durable as their similarities; that these differences are not divagations from a European norm, but structures eminently worth knowing about for their own sake. In the world that is coming, if you can't navigate difference, you've had it.

Thus, if multiculturalism is about learning to see through borders, I'm all in favor of it. Americans have a real problem in imagining the rest of the world. They are not the only ones—most things are foreign to most people—but considering the variety of national origins represented in their vast society, its incuriosity and proneness to stereotype can still surprise the foreigner, even (in my case) after twenty years' residence in the U.S. For example: If white Americans still have difficulty seeing blacks, what of Arabs? Like everyone else, I watched the Gulf War on television, read about it in the press, and saw how that conflict brought to an ugly climax America's long-implanted habit of hostile ignorance about the Arab world, past and present. Rarely did one get an indication from the media, let alone from politicians, that the realities of Islamic culture (both past and present) were anything other than a history of fanaticism. Instead, a succession of pundits came forth to assure the public that Arabs were basically a bunch of volatile religious maniacs, hostage-takers, sons of thornbush and dune whose whole past disposed them against intercourse with more civilized states. Modern Islamic fundamentalism filled the screen with screaming mouths and waving arms; of the Islamic past—let alone present-day Arab dissent from fundamentalist xenophobia and militarism—one heard much less. It was as though Americans were being fed an amplified, updated version of the views on Islam held by Ferdinand and Isabella in the 15th century. The core message was that Arabs were not just uncivilized, but *uncivilizable*. In its perverse way, this represented a victory for the mullahs and for Saddam Hussein—in American eyes, everything in the Arab world that contradicted their cruelties and eschatological manias was blotted out, so that they were left in full possession of the field.

But to treat Islamic culture and history as a mere prelude to today's fanaticism gets us nowhere. It is like reading a French Gothic cathedral in terms of such modern Christians as Jimmy Swaggart or Pat Robertson. Historically, Islam the Destroyer is a myth. Without Arab scholars, our mathematics would not exist and only a fraction of the Greek intellectual heritage would have come down to us. Medieval Rome was a scavengers' village compared with medieval Baghdad. Without the Arab invasion of southern Spain or *el-Andalus* in the 8th century, which produced the farthest westward expansion of the Islamic empire run by the Abbasid dynasty from Baghdad, the culture of southern Europe would be unimaginably poorer. Hispano-Arabic Andalusia, between the 12th and 15th centuries, was a brilliant "multicultural" civilization, built over the ruins (and incorporating the half-lost motifs) of ancient Roman colonies, mingling Western with middle-Eastern forms, glorious in its lyric invention and adaptive tolerance. What architecture surpasses that of the Alhambra in Granada, or the Great Mosque of Córdoba? *Mestizaje es grandeza:* mixture is greatness.

The conservative fear of mixture is tinged with paranoid exaggeration. One need only suggest that "history from below"—a phrase invented by the theologian Dietrich Bonhoeffer, in the black days of Europe in 1942, to denote a possible history of "those who suffer"—clearly has some moral and educational point to it, and the chorus begins. Lay aside Plato and pick up a copy of Rigoberta Menchu, and suddenly there's William Bennett, with his big black boots on, announcing that it's closing time in the gardens of Western Civ. "It is a given that the enemy of justice and humanity is Western man," sneers Dorothy Rabinowitz, editorial writer for the *Wall Street Journal*.

What is so fragile about Western Civ? And conversely, what is so radical about multiculturalism, which in America means an improved understanding of the art, literature, history and values of cultures other than the dominant Anglo-Jewish one? Writers and academics are not the only people to recognize that multiculturalism is the wave of the future. But they are probably the only ones (apart from their conservative opponents, for here, too, extremes meet) to have convinced themselves that it poses a threat to capitalism. The capitalists themselves know that it does not. Ted Turner's decision, a few years ago, to ban the word "foreign" from global CNN newscasts was a more significant moment in the multicultural enterprise than all the papers on Self and Other that have ever been read at the Modern Language Association's jamborees. For, as the cultural critic David Rieff has pointed out,[3]

> the more one reads in academic multiculturalist journals and in business publications, the more one contrasts the speeches of CEOs and the speech of noted multiculturalist academics, the more one is struck by the similarities in the ways they view the world. Far from standing in implacable intellectual opposition to one another, both groups see the same racial and gender transformation in the demographic makeup of the country and the workforce; both emphasize the importance of women, and of the need to change the workplace in such a way as to make it more hospitable to women; and both insist that it is no longer possible to speak of the United States as some fixed, autarchic entity, and emphasize world over nation.

Unhappily, you do not have to listen very long to the arguments on the other side before sensing that, in quite a few of its proponents' minds, multiculturalism means something less than genuine curiosity about other cultural forms. The first casualty of this is the idea of Europe itself—for how can anyone with the slightest acquaintance with the enormous, rich, contradictory range of European literature and thought presume that it forms one solid "Eurocentric" mass, "as if," in Russell Jacoby's words, "Adolf Hitler and Anne Frank represented the same world"? We hear people invoke something they call Latin-American culture (as distinct from the "repressive" culture of the Anglo) without realizing what coarse generalizations the phrase implies. There is no "Latin-American literature" as such, any more than there is a place called "Asia" with a common literature that somehow connects the *Ramayana,* the works of Confucius and the *Pillow-Book of Sei Shonagon.* There are only the cultures of various and distinct Latin-American countries, diverse in themselves, drawing on common pools of imagery—the vast reservoir of Roman Catholicism, for instance—but inflected by their own political and racial histories, different senses of nationhood and identity, and different languages. All are the products of long, intense, unpredictable hybridization between three continents, Africa, Europe and America—the process which, more and more, is seen at the center of "Eurocentric" culture as well. For example, is it possible to speak of a single literary "Portuguese language"? Instead of one "pure" Portuguese tongue, there are several, all the result of colonialization and mixture. There is the stem language of Portugal itself, in which Camoens wrote his epic *Os Lusiades.* But then there is Brazilian Portuguese too, transformed by African and Indian borrowings that break with the colonizers' grammar and usage. There is the Portuguese of Angola; the Portuguese of Mozambique, mingled with Hindi; the Portuguese of Cabo Verde, created as a literary idiom by the poet Jorge Barbosa, and that of Guinea Bissau. Each one is the base of a distinctive literature and to speak, like so many Spaniards and North Americans, of a generality called "Latin-American writing" is to utter an empty abstraction.

What is more, many "radicals" seem to assume that, in looking at other cultures under the rubric of "multiculturalism," one should gaze mainly at their versions of Marxism, "liberation struggle," and so forth. But is this not just another Eurocentric caricature, to be asked to admire in other countries and cultures the ideological forms they have borrowed, recently, from the West? If this enthusiasm for Marxist reenactments in Africa, Asia and the Middle East is not Eurocentrism, what is? When Maoism was fashionable in the West, it was completely misunderstood by its groupies—not only because they failed to see what a hideous tyranny it was, but because they imagined it was new, which was the greatest illusion of all. The history, civilization and thought of China is so old and continuous that its own version of Stalinist oligarchical collectivism, devised by Mao Tse-tung and imposed less than fifty years ago, is no more than a tiny blip in six millennia of recorded Chinese history. Maoism cannot be understood except as a reappearance, in Marx-face, of the archaic Chinese cult of the immutable god-emperor that reached its apogee under the Qing in the late 18th century. All too often, what poses as "radical multiculturalism" exists in an ignorance of other cultures as profound as that of a West Coast car-salesman newly appointed as the U.S. Ambassador to Somewherestan in the 60s.

III

In fact, it means separatism. It alleges that European institutions and mental structures are inherently oppressive, and that non-Eurocentric ones are not—a dubious idea, to say the least. The sense of disappointment and frustration with formal politics has gone down into culture, stuck there and festered. It has caused many people to view the arts mainly as a field of power, since they have so little power elsewhere. Thus they also become an arena for complaint about rights.

This process has gravely distorted current ideas about the political capacity of the arts, just at the moment when—due to the pervasiveness of mass media—they have reached their nadir of real political effect. The frame of mind this creates is a rich compost for phantom cultural issues, and a poor environment for clear thought about real ones.

One example is the inconclusive debate over "The Canon," that oppressive Big Bertha whose muzzle is trained over the battlements of Western Civ at the black, the gay, and the female. The Canon, we're told, is a list of books by dead Europeans—Shakespeare and Dante and Tolstoy and Dostoievsky and Stendhal and John Donne and T. S. Eliot . . . you know, *them*, the pale patriarchal penis people. I didn't even know there *was* a Canon until long after I got to the States, and by then it was too late. Mortimer Adler was unknown in Australia. At home, we didn't have a shelf of Great Books of the West bound in hand-tooled naugahyde. We just had a lot of shelves filled with a lot of books in no particular order, ranging from *Paradise Lost* to *Andrew Lang's Purple Book of Fairy Stories,* from Shakespeare to our national doggerelist Banjo Patterson, from Xenophon's *Anabasis* to *Kim, The Jungle Book*—the original, so utterly different from the boorish and bowdlerized Disney version which is all that most kids get today—and *The Hunting of the Snark.* Hence the fatal eclectism of my childish reading habits. Nobody told me that one kind of book drove out another.

Those who complain about the Canon think it creates readers who will never read anything else.

If only! What they don't want to admit, at least not publicly, is that most American students don't read much anyway and quite a few, left to their own devices, would not read at all.

Their moronic national babysitter, the television set, took care of that. In 1991, the majority of American households (60 percent, the same as in Spain) did not buy one single book. Before long, Americans will think of the time when people sat at home and read books for their own sake, discursively and sometimes even aloud to one another, as a lost era—the way we now see rural quilting-bees in the 1870s. No American university can *assume* that its first-year students are literate in a more than technical sense. Perhaps they never could. But they certainly can't now. It is hard to exaggerate the narrowness of reference, the indifference to reading, the lightly dimpled cultural shallowness of many young products of American TV culture, even the privileged ones.

At universities which charge $22,000 a year for the continuing education of young Carmen or Peter, fine-arts and humanities teachers are busily making it clear to their charges that elitism is the pox of Western culture, and that it is wrong to develop much of a critical sense lest they catch it. America's peculiar convulsions over the academic literary canon come less from a passionate interest in writing, than from notions of what is or is not therapeutic.

Now this, as the writer Katha Pollitt recently pointed

out,[4] gives much of the debate over the Canon its peculiarly airless and futile quality. The underlying assumption, she argues,

> is that the books on the list are the only ones that are going to be read, and if the list is dropped no books are going to be read. Becoming a textbook is a book's only chance; all sides take that for granted. And so all agree not to mention certain things . . . For example, that if you have read only 25, or 50, or 100 books, you can't understand them, however well chosen they are. And that if you don't have an independent reading life— and very few students do—you won't *like* reading the books on the list and will forget them the moment you finish them.

The quarrel over the Canon reflects the sturdy assumption that works of art are or ought to be therapeutic. Imbibe the *Republic* or *Phaedo* at nineteen, and you will be one kind of person; study *Jane Eyre* or *Mrs. Dalloway* or the poetry of Aphra Behn, and you will be another; read Amiri Baraka or *The Color Purple* or the writings of Wole Soyinka, and you will be a third. This happens, or is supposed to happen, because the author, whether it's Plato or Alice Walker, becomes a "role model" for the reader, whose imitative faculties are roused by the writer's imaginative ones. If you read Evelyn Waugh before Franz Fanon you may become a racist (if white), or (if black) suffer an attack of the bends through sudden decompression of self-esteem. For in the literary zero-sum game of Canon talk, if you read X it means that you don't read Y.

In theory, all good liberals are for the widest access to every "serious" text for everyone. In practice we are not always so sure, because writers do in fact want to move us, to change our viewpoint on some aspect of life, great or small; and what do you do with a writer of indubitable gifts, even of genius, whose views are by any reasonable standards repellent? What about Céline, for instance, whose imaginative power and poisonous anti-Semitism were both impelled by his rage against French bourgeois life, inextricably twined, so that you cannot *have* the pitiless talent without the Jew-hating? Or, as Simone de Beauvoir asked in the title of an essay, "Must We Burn Sade?"—Sade, the republican as absolute anti-democrat, the writer who imagined his fellow human beings as mere victims, passive instruments for the sovereign will of pleasure in a sealed, absolutist universe where "Cruelty is one of the most natural human feelings, one of the sweetest of man's inclinations, one of the most intense he has received from nature"? Literature isn't a nice normalizing course of treatment whose purpose is to guide and cuff us into becoming better citizens of whatever republic we are reading in.

This occasionally seems to escape the intellectuals of both sides in America. When Norman Podhoretz wrote that "As the transmitter of the canon . . . the humanities have traditionally instilled a sense of the value of the democratic traditions we have inherited," one wonders what he meant. For every writer who praised "democratic traditions," another feared and distrusted them—starting with Plato. Shakespeare, for instance, with his contempt for the fickle unprincipled mob, so vividly evoked in *Julius Caesar* and in Coriolanus' speech to the plebeians:

> You common cry of curs, whose breath I hate
> As reek o' th' rotten fens, whose loves I prize

As the dead carcasses of unburied men
That do corrupt my air: I banish you.

Or Dryden, to whom the fall of kings and the stirrings of egalitarianism in 17th-century England meant hateful regression into "nature's state, where all have right to all." Or Baudelaire: "We have all of us got the republican spirit in our veins, as we have the pox in our bones: we are democratized and syphilized." Or Nietzsche, or Pound, or Lawrence, or Yeats ("All that was sung / All that was said in Ireland is a lie / Bred out of the contagion of the throng")—the list of notable democracy-haters fills quite a lot of any literary canon you care to invent.

It would also include some of those writers whom neo-conservatives like to hold up as models of critical probity: Matthew Arnold, for instance, who believed universities should preserve "the best that has been thought and said," but as an *antidote* to the spreading values of liberal democracy. Or T. S. Eliot—he of the old *Criterion*—who trusted democracy about as much as he liked Jews, and took up Matthew Arnold's project of reinforcing the mystique of monarchy and High Anglicanism against erosion by democratic values. Were not Eliot's elevation of Spenser the court poet, and his hostility to Milton the republican and regicide, *politically* inspired? Both Eliot and Leavis wanted to dislodge Milton from the Canon altogether, a task comparable to pushing a beached whale back in the surf on a falling tide. But it was a very edited Eliot we got from the neo-conservatives: an Eliot with the monarchist flatulence tuned down (the way the brutal side of 18th-century English life was left discreetly unexplored by the catalogues of drop-dead Stately Home museum shows in the 80s, like *Treasure Houses of Great Britain*). The anti-Semitism of this Eliot tends to be kept in the wings too, perhaps because it is uncomfortably close to modern conservative arguments for the integrity of the Canon: some intruders dilute the real right wholeness of Western culture, for (he wrote in *After Strange Gods*) "What is still more important is unity of religious background; and reasons of race and religion combine to make any large number of free-thinking Jews undesirable."

It is the habit of neo-conservatives to claim, when attacking "politicized" readings of literature, that they themselves represent *un*political readings, a view of history, novels, drama and poetry that is not contaminated by ideology. "Disinterested" is the code-word.

Yet the immense republic of literature contains everything—and its opposite. I have read a lot of books in the last forty-five years, since I became a conscious and addicted reader at the age of about nine. But when I try to imagine the number of books I have not read, and perhaps should have, and now probably never will, I feel giddy and ashamed.

The first trouble with a rigid, exclusionary canon of Great Writing is that it can never be complete: it is always in some sense a prosthetic device, a pedagogical aid whose limitations become clearer when it is moved outside the peculiar course-requirements of the university.

The second is that, like a museum full of beautiful paintings run by curators too timid to expand the collection, it will ossify.

The third is that its defensive stance attracts hostility, turning its own contents into objects of resentment and thus making them harder to approach.

The critic Frederick Crews makes the case that neo-conservatives like Allan Bloom, William Bennett and Roger Kimball are "cultural nostalgics" who

> implicitly subscribe to a "transfusion" model of education, whereby the stored-up wisdom of the classics is considered a kind of plasma that will drip beneficially into our veins if we only stay sufficiently passive in its presence. My own notion of learning is entirely different. I want keen debate, not reverence for great books; historical consciousness and self-reflection, not supposedly timeless values; and continual expansion of our national canon to match a necessarily unsettled sense of who "we" are and what we ultimately care about . . . a certain amount of turmoil surrounding the canon should be taken in stride. In my view there can be no such thing as a sacrosanct text, an innately civilizing idea, or an altogether disinterested literary critic.[5]

Crews is surely right; and the idea that one can construct a hierarchy of Timeless Values, and maintain it against the vicissitudes of the present (favorite metaphors, navigational: polestar, lighthouse, anchor in the tide, etcetera) is wrong. But how could this be construed as an argument for junking the classics? To see why immutability doesn't work, we have to immerse ourselves in the past as well as the limiting present, thereby (with luck and hard work) grasping at least as many of the "canonical" works, and internalizing them as deeply, as we could if we *believed* in the need for a strict canon. If we do this, we see—among other things—that the history of literature is one of continuous inclusion and subversion, that literary taste has rarely stood still for long, and that there is no reason to expect it to do so now. Especially not now, given the profoundly unsettled state of American culture, the crises of cultural identity that come with the dissolution of the binary world held in place for forty years by the left and right jaws of the Cold War's iron clamp. The key words must be "both/and," not "either/or."

Conservatives may not want us to get into this maze, but some lumpen-radical assumptions won't get us through it. One is the remedial fantasy of culture—the notion, mentioned above, that we necessarily become what we read. But what could be more stultifying than to sentence a student to rehearse what his teacher believes is culturally appropriate to his race, gender or class, and ignore the rest? Another is distrust of the dead, as in "dead white European male." I take it for granted that some books are deeper, wider, fuller than others, and more necessary to an understanding of our culture and ourselves. They remain so, long after their authors are dead. Those who parrot phrases like "dead white male" might reflect that, in writing, death is relative: Lord Rochester is as dead as Sappho, though by no means as moribund as Brett Easton Ellis or Andrea Dworkin. Statistically, most authors *are* dead, but some of them continue to speak to us with a vividness and moral urgency which few of the living can rival. And the more we read, the more writers—living and dead— we find who do so, which is why the Canon is not a fortress but a permeable membrane.

Where does this distrust of the dead come from? Perhaps it is an echo from the 1960s, when that squalid hustler Jerry Rubin exhorted the youth of America not to trust anyone over thirty; but more likely, it is an aspect of the disparagement of cultural memory that pervades the United States. Ezra Pound's exhortation to "MAKE IT NEW" hangs over all

American culture, including Canon debates. But it is misunderstood. Pound never meant it as a sign that the present erases the past. The phrase fascinated him because he believed it had been written on the bathtub of the Ch'ing Emperor and that it was an injunction to carry the work of the past, constantly refreshed, into the present: the "it" is tradition itself:

> Tching . . .
> . . . wrote MAKE IT NEW
> on his bathtub
>   Day by day make it new
> cut underbrush,
> pile the logs
> keep it growing.

Reading is *expansive,* not exclusive. If Caribbean, African, Arab and Indian writers get more attention today, if the Booker prize is won by Ben Okri from Nigeria or Peter Carey from Sydney, if readers approach the work of women and blacks without prejudice and without the sense of tiptoeing up on a special case, our shared culture grows and rejoices. We learn how other kinds of cultural consciousness can occupy the speaking center of literary forms. But how could this conceivably be a reason for not reading *Eugene Onegin* or Pope's *Epistle to Lord Burlington*?

IV

The sense of quality, of style, of measure is not an imposition bearing on literature from the domain of class, race or gender. It lives independently of group stereotypes. Every writer carries in his or her mind an invisible tribunal of dead writers, whose appointment is an imaginative act and not merely a browbeaten response to some notion of authority. This tribunal sits in judgment on our own work. We intuit our standards from it. From its unenforceable verdict, there is no appeal. None of our tricks—not our fetishization of the personal, not our attempts to shift the aesthetic into the political, not our exhausted fictions of avant-gardism—will make it go away. Not if we are frank with ourselves. If the tribunal weren't there, every first draft would be a final manuscript. You can't fool Mother Culture.

The *Odyssey* can't mean exactly the same things to us that it meant to a reader in first-century Alexandria, or to one in 17th-century France. But it continues to *mean,* to irradiate the mind of the willing and receptive reader with the vast light of imaginative possibility. You can't get around this with the notion that students should only be taught what is, in the cant phrase, "relevant to their experience: writing *creates* experience. We have all read about, and some have met, indignant students and teachers wanting to know why we should bother with Homer, since he is a dead white male and could have nothing to say to a live black female.

When I hear such things I think of Derek Walcott's *Omeros.* Walcott, winner of the 1992 Nobel for literature, is black and divides his time between Harvard and the Caribbean island of Saint Lucia. *Omeros* is that uncommon event, a long reflective and narrative poem, dense with exquisite observation, thronged with characters and cast in the epic form. It defies all the conventions of minimalist writing. It takes the Homeric frame of Ulysses' voyage and conflates it with the central event of black history in the New World, the shipment

of slaves across the Atlantic, to which the poet owes his ulti-
mate identity. And the question, what relevance can Homer
have to me? is answered quite early on when the narrator is
talking to a Greek girl, pining for her own Aegean islands, as
he is for the Caribbean. She has on a shelf a head of Homer.

"O-meros," she laughed. "That's what we call him in Greek, . . ."

I felt the foam head watching as I stroked an arm, as
cold as its marble, then the shoulders in winter light
in the studio attic. I said, "Omeros,"

and *O* was the conch-shell's invocation, *mer* was
both mother and sea in our Antillean patois,
os, a grey bone, and the white surf as it crashes

and spreads its sibilant collar on a lace shore.
Omeros was the crunch of dry leaves, and the washes
that echoed from a cave-mouth when the tide has ebbed.

The name stayed in my mouth . . .

So should it, and many other names, stay in ours, whatever
our ethnic origin or country of birth. They will not be dispelled by facile chitchat about Dead White Males versus politically OK living writers. On this point, I can't do better than
quote Edward Saïd, whose books *Orientalism* and *Culture
and Imperialism* are such key works of recent transcultural
thought. "These clamorous dismissals and swooping asser-
tions," Saïd writes,

are in fact caricatural reductions of what the great revisionary
gestures of feminism, subaltern or black studies, and anti-imperi-
alist resistance originally intended. For such gestures it was never

a matter of replacing one set of authorities and dogmas with another, nor of substituting one center for another. It was always a matter of opening and participating in a central strand of intellectual and cultural effort and of showing what had always been, though indiscernibly, a part of it, like the work of women, or of blacks . . . but which had been either denied or derogated.[6]

That is why, as a writer, I reject not only the poststructuralist argument that all writing is indeterminate, but also the renewed attempt to judge writing in terms of its presumed social virtue. Through it, one enters a strange, nostalgic, Marxist never-never land, where all the most retrograde phantoms of Literature as Instrument of Social Utility are trotted forth. Thus one finds the new *Columbia History of the American Novel* declaring Harriet Beecher Stowe a better novelist than Melville because she was a woman and "socially constructive," because *Uncle Tom's Cabin* helped rouse Americans against slavery . . . whereas the captain of the *Pequod* was a symbol of laissez-faire capitalist individualism with a bad attitude to whales.

With the same argument you can claim that an artist like William Gropper, who drew those stirring cartoons of fat capitalists in top hats for the *New Masses* sixty years ago, may have something over an artist like Edward Hopper, who didn't care a plugged nickel for community and was always painting those figures in lonely rooms in such a way that you can't be absolutely sure whether he was criticizing alienation or affirming the virtues of solitude.

These backward habits of judging writers in terms of their presumed ability to improve social consciousness may be tough luck for snobbish Proust and depressive Leopardi, for Henry James the closet case and Montaigne the son of bourgeois privilege. But they are even tougher for the students, who come away with the impression that the correct response to a text is to run a crude political propriety-meter over it and then let fly with a wad of stereotyped moralizing. "Boy, Professor Peach really did a job of unmasking the hierarchical assumptions in Dante last week, all those circles and stuff, you shoulda been there."

Politics ought not be all-pervasive. Indeed, one of the first conditions of freedom is to discover the line beyond which politics may not go, and literature is one of the means by which the young (and the old) find this out. Some works of art have an overt political content; many carry subliminal political messages, embedded in their framework. But it is remarkably naive to suppose that these messages exhaust the content of the art as art, or ultimately determine its value. Why, then, the fashion for judging art in political terms? Probably, people teach it because it is easy to teach. It revives the illusion that works of art carry social meaning the way trucks carry coal. It divides the sprawling republic of literature neatly into goodies and baddies, and relieves the student of the burden of imaginative empathy, the difficulties of aesthetic discrimination. It enables these scholars, with their tin ears, schematized minds and tapioca prose, to henpeck dead writers for their lack of conformity to the current fashions in "oppression studies"—and to fool themselves and their equally nostalgic colleagues into thinking that they are all on the barricades.

Yet when the Iranian mullahs pronounced their *fatwa* against a live writer, Salman Rushdie, for "blasphemy" against Islam, fixing a price on his head for writing words they didn't like, academe hardly broke its silence. American academics failed to collectively protest this obscenity for two reasons.

First, they feared their own campuses might become the targets of Islamic terrorists. Second, the more politically correct among them felt it was wrong to criticize a Muslim country, no matter what it did. At home in America, such folk knew it was the height of sexist impropriety to refer to a young female as a "girl" instead of a "woman." Abroad in Teheran, however, it was more or less OK for a cabal of regressive theocratic bigots to insist on the chador, to cut off thieves' hands and put out the eyes of offenders on TV, and to murder novelists as State policy. Oppression is what we do in the West. What they do in the Middle East is "their culture." Though of course we don't go along with everything the mobs—correction, the masses—of Iran say or do, we have to recognize that this culture is indeed theirs, not ours, and that the objective circumstances of anti-Arab racism in these Eurocentric United States would make a protest from the lit department seem like a caving-in to the values of the Republicans, who have used the often regrettable excesses of Islamic fundamentalism, which must be seen within a global context of Western aggression against Third World peoples, as a pretext for . . . but one gets the drift.

V

It's in the area of history that PC has scored its largest successes.

The reading of history is never static. Revise we historians must. There is no such thing as the last word. And who could doubt that there is still much to revise in the story of the

European conquest of North and South America that we inherited? Its scheme was imperial: the epic advance of Civilization against Barbarism: the conquistador brings the Cross and the sword, the red man shrinks back before the cavalry and the railroad. Manifest Destiny. The white American myth of the 19th century. The notion that all historians propagated this triumphalist myth uncritically is quite false: you have only to read Parkman or Prescott to realize that. But after the myth sank from the histories deep into popular culture, it became a potent justification for the plunder, murder and enslavement of peoples, and the wreckage of nature.

So now, in reaction to it, comes the manufacture of its opposite myth. European man, once the hero of the conquest of the Americas, now becomes its demon; and the victims, who cannot be brought back to life, are canonized. On either side of the divide between Euro and native, historians stand ready with tar-brush and gold leaf, and instead of the wicked old stereotypes we have a whole new outfit of equally misleading ones. Our predecessors made a hero, almost a saint, of Christopher Columbus. He has monuments from Barcelona to the Antilles (which he discovered, though it is not known which island he actually landed on) and all over North America, the mainland he never glimpsed. To Europeans and North Americans in 1892, he was Manifest Destiny in tights, surrounded by deposits of pious folklore, such as Washington Irving's story about Columbus and the egg or the fiction that Queen Isabella pawned her jewels, which had actually been hocked long before to pay for cannon, in order to finance his voyages. Whereas a PC book like Kirkpatrick Sale's *The Conquest of Paradise* makes him more like Hitler in a caravel, grasping and filled with apocalyptic fancies, landing like a virus among the innocent people of the New World.

This new stereotype, a rebirth of Rousseauist notions about the Noble Savage, brings a new outfit of double standards into play. Thus the Taino of Puerto Rico become innocent creatures living in a state of classless nature, like hippies in Vermont when Kirkpatrick Sale and I were young, whereas in fact they liked to be carried around in litters by their slaves. If only the people of the Americas, from Patagonia to the Great Lakes, had not been conquered by the Europeans, would they not still be in bliss? Are we not so much worse than they?

Well, yes, up to a point. The arrival of the Spaniards in the Americas was an unutterable catastrophe for the peoples of South America and the Caribbean, as the imperial push of Anglos through North America was for its native tribes. If one accepts the figures presented by David Stannard in his recent book, *American Holocaust: Columbus and the Conquest of the New World,* the slaughter occasioned by the Spanish *conquista* in Peru and Chile may have run as high as 95 percent of the population, perhaps ten million souls; and the total human population loss of the Western hemisphere may have reached one hundred million in the first two centuries after European arrival. If so, that would be the worst genocide in human history, far surpassing Hitler's.

Can we say Columbus bears the guilt for this? In a general and emblematic way, yes, for he led Europe to America. In terms of personal guilt, no, for he did not plan these gigantic massacres by sword and disease; he had, for instance, no more knowledge of the epidemiology of swine influenza (the probable cause of the destruction of the people of Hispaniola within ten years of his arrival) than the Arawaks themselves did. For all that, he remains the greatest of all Atlantic explorers. His only rival in history was Captain James Cook, as brave a man but a far more rational and humane one, who added most of the Pacific and Antarctic Oceans to the European horizon nearly three centuries later. Cook is my hero; Columbus is white America's ex-hero. Cook seems closer to us because he was an Englishman of the Enlightenment, and we still to some degree speak his moral language. Columbus is very remote, because he came from an eschatological culture, that of 15th-century Spain, whose God-stricken obsessions we do not share. In Cook's time there was a difference, which his own achievements express, between discovery and conquest. In Columbus's time there was none.

What would have happened if the peoples of the western Atlantic had not been conquered by eschatological brutes? The speculation is existentially meaningless, because America *was* overrun by these imperfect and cruel beings who imposed their own cultures, Spanish and then English and French, on the existing ones. If Columbus had not opened the route to the Caribbean, someone else—Spanish, Portuguese, Italian, English—would have done it a few years later, and the results for the societies and ecology of the Americas would have been much the same. To expect Mayans, or modern American Indians, to celebrate 1992 is unreasonable; as an Australian Aboriginal remarked at the time of our bicentenary in 1988, you might as well ask Jews to celebrate Hitler's centenary, which was due the next year, 1989.

But the historical evidence also shows that the peoples of the Americas had been doing very nicely for centuries and probably for millennia, when it came to murder, torture, materialism, ecocide, enslavement and sexist hegemony. We may worry about the fate of the spotted owl, but the first men to arrive in prehistoric north America did not seem to have any qualms about their extinction of its megafauna, which they accomplished in short order. The civilization of the Maya, the greatest to flourish in Central America before Columbus, reached its peak between 250 and 900 A.D., at which point a puzzling event called the Mayan Hiatus occurred. It collapsed. Nobody from outside had conquered it. However, recent digs and the slow work of deciphering glyphs, particularly at the site of Dos Pilas in Guatemala, indicate that the classic period of the Maya was ruined by a continuous state of war between local rulers that began around 700 A.D. and devoured the whole economy and ecology of the Mayan empire by the 10th century. The Mayans fell by self-induced ecological collapse, caused by a devotion to unwinnable wars which was itself sustained by an obsession with ideology—the ideology of the transcendent god-king, viewed by his limestone-toting helots as the embodiment of the whole universe.

Pre-Columbian Meso-America was not the Shangri-la that anti-Columbians would like it to be. You cannot climb the Pyramid of the Sun at Teotihuacán near Mexico City and look down the vast symmetrical perspective of the Avenue of the Dead, abandoned in the 8th century for reasons we know nothing about, without sensing that the society that built them was a theocratic ant-state whose rigidity might have made Albert Speer faint. And try staring at the fangs of the Feathered Serpent and talking about the benign pastoral quality of life before whitey arrived. Aztec culture was messianic and invasive and imperialistic; it had been so ever since the Aztecs came down from the north, under the command of a charismatic ruler whose name translates as Hummingbird-on-the-Left, and slaughtered or enslaved the resident people around what is now Mexico City. I suppose the survivors could be glad there was no Hummingbird-on-the-Right. But by now, it is anachronistic to condemn or to justify the destruction of Aztec society by the Spanish *conquista*. It was an evil fate to be enslaved by 16th-century Spanish regidors. But it was no joke to be one of the countless thousands whose hearts were ripped out by the Aztec priests of Tenochtitlán in order that the sun might rise in the morning. The Spanish burned nearly all the written records of Aztec history, except for a few codices. But the Aztecs, when they conquered central Mexico, also destroyed all the records of the previous societies, so that there could be no history before theirs.

The need for absolute goodies and absolute baddies runs deep in us, but it drags history into propaganda and denies the humanity of the dead: their sins, their virtues, their efforts, their failures. To preserve complexity, and not flatten it under the weight of anachronistic moralizing, is part of the historian's task. One could do worse than remember the advice of the Brazilian novelist Jorge Amado, reflecting on the 500th anniversary of Columbus and the conquest of the New World: for some, he wrote, it means

> the epic of discovery, the meeting of two worlds; for others, the infamy of the *conquista* and of genocide. . . . One must set up and compare appearances and differences, because only in this way, by understanding what was great and will be an eternal glory, by disclosing what was wretched and will be a perpetual shame, only thus, in reflection and understanding, can we both celebrate the epic and condemn the massacre, neither of which expunges the other. We are the product of both—the mixed peoples of America.[7]

Surprises crackle, like electric arcs, between the interfaces of culture. These interfaces are where history now seeks itself;

they will be the historical sites of the future. You cannot remake the past in the name of affirmative action. But you can find narratives that haven't been written, histories of people and groups that have been distorted or ignored, and refresh history by bringing them in. That is why, in the last twenty-five years, so much of the vitality of written history has come from the left. When you read the work of the black Caribbean historian C. L. R. James, you see a part of the world break its traditional silence—a silence not of its own choosing, but *imposed* on it by earlier imperial writers. Part of my own education as a writer, twenty years ago, was reading E. P. Thompson's *The Making of the English Working Class,* which showed me how history might be constructed from below, assembling and making sense of the officially ignored experiences of workers whose stories, in more doctrinaire hands, might have become lost in generalizations about class rather than brought to life in all their particularity. The list of books inspired by Thompson's masterpiece would be long, and certainly I know that *The Fatal Shore* was my attempt to apply this lesson to the submerged story of the Australian convicts. What I found useless, by contrast, was the abstract theorizing about prison and power in texts that became sacred in American academe in the early 80s, such as Michel Foucault's *Discipline and Punish.* In his ruminations about Jeremy Bentham's theory of the Panopticon, or total-surveillance prison, Foucault contrived to do exactly what he blamed the State for doing in real life: ignore the experience of prisoners themselves, hardly even bother to consult evidence about it, lest it disturb the autocratic, cuckoo-clock self-referentiality of his own theoretical constructs. Foucault's American admirers fail to see what an authoritarian he was, deep in the closet.

History, above all, must be concerned with human life as

it has been lived, to the extent that it can be discovered through the filters of the past. You do not have to be a Marxist to appreciate the truth of Eric Hobsbawm's claim that the most widely recognized achievement of radical history "has been to win a place for the history of ordinary people, common men and women." In America, this work necessarily includes the histories of blacks and other minorities, which tend to break down complacent nationalist readings of the American past. One of the outstanding exemplars of such work was the late Herbert Gutman (1928–85), in *The Black Family in Slavery and Freedom 1750–1925*. Gutman was one of a now uncommon breed, the historian who wants to take his work before a general public, showing the complex realities of the "underside of history" in terms just as accessible to non-specialist readers as the Great-Men histories of elites had once been. His American Social History Project was an act of public reclamation of the sort that cuts no ice with New Left historians today; not "theoretical" enough, too "populist." One also thinks of Eugene Genovese's work on slavery, or Eric Foner's on Reconstruction, or Leon Litwack's superb book on the experiences of black Americans after emancipation, *Been in the Storm So Long*. Or, more recently, of Nicholas Lemann's story of the great northward migration of blacks to Illinois, *The Promised Land*. The need for such studies would have been disputed by American historians two generations ago. Today, they seem fundamental. For as Litwack remarked in his presidential address to the Organization of American Historians in 1987: "No group of scholars was more deeply implicated in the miseducation of American youth and did more to shape the thinking of generations of Americans about race and blacks than historians."

Likewise, the history of the frontier can never be the same as it was for our grandparents. Their idea of an America defined by frontier experience grew from an immensely influential paper read by Frederick Jackson Turner to the American Historical Association in 1893: "The Significance of the Frontier in American History." In it, Turner argued that "the existence of an area of free land, its continuous recession, and the advance of American settlement westward, explain American development." This was in direct contradiction to earlier (Puritan-based) historians who wrote as though everything in America, and especially the values and criteria by which events are interpreted and through which we try to answer the crucial question "Whose history?," emanated from New England. But for more than two decades now Turner's scheme, which is essentially that of Manifest Destiny, the American version of English imperial history with the whites advancing into an unowned "wilderness" (*terra nullius* or "no man's land," as 18th-century colonizers of the Pacific used to say) has been criticized, modified and outright rejected by newer Western historians. To view this as simple debunking of the heroic West—an Oedipal assault on the myths of popular culture by writers who don't like the West—is very far from the truth. Rather, the object is twofold: on one hand to find a real historical West under the mythic West, and on the other to study the history of the "mythic West" as a construction of images and stereotypes—how they were created and fostered, how they came to dominate popular culture. Any effort to discover the historical realities of the West, historians now acknowledge, must begin with multiculturalism: that is, above all, by recognizing that the West was not a *terra nullius* into which the whites marched; that it was a highly charged arena in which various cultures, the invading Anglo-American and the already resident Indian and Spanish, impacted on one another, never with simple results. Nor can the drama and complexity of the West be understood without seeing how persistent and resilient the values, beliefs and cultural forms of the "vanquished" still are, despite long efforts by the Anglo "victors" both to suppress them and to deny the suppression itself with the more comfortable notion that they just faded away. Exactly the same process took place in Australia, with its 19th-century belief in "the passing of the Aborigine," so curiously in accord with the *fin-de-siècle*'s favored literary tropes of mist, wraiths and suggestive indistinctness.

It is true that revisions of Western history can embarrass cherished myths. To take only one of many examples: the West is archetypally the place where Big Government is distrusted, the land of the independent man going it alone. Yet much of it—states like Arizona, for instance—has depended, not marginally or occasionally but always and totally, on Federal money from Washington for its economic existence. The Southwestern states could never have been settled at their present human density without immense expenditure of government funds on water-engineering. They are less the John Wayne than the Welfare Queen of American development.

What we see in the "new" history, and in the once vocal but now fading resistance to it, is a revival of the conflict over race and class ownership of historical writing that troubled American academe in the 1930s and again in the 1950s. In his excellent survey *The Great Multicultural Debate,* the historian Gary B. Nash showed how, after World War I, Jewish scholars had to struggle for a place in the American historical profession, considered a fief of the brahmin Wasp; and how resistance to their intrusion was still strong enough in the early 1960s for Carl Bridenbaugh, the president of the American Historical Association, to complain that "many of the younger practitioners of our craft . . . are products of lower middle-class or foreign origins, and their emotions not infrequently get in the way of historical reconstruction." But in due course it became clear even to the Bridenbaughs that, if America were to understand the meaning of its 19th-century immigrations—the greatest impaction of diverse peoples on a single state in all recorded history, with perhaps thirty-five million people coming to North America in seventy years—those "products of . . . foreign origins," Wasp code for Jews, Italians and other irrational beings, might have some light to cast on it. Due to the pressure of school boards in cities with large black and Hispanic populations, secondary-school textbooks in the 1960s were somewhat revised, in the direction of seeing America as a multiracial and multicultural society. But mono-culturalist history is tenacious, and conservatives love it; through the 70s and 80s, the same kind of pressures that fundamentalists applied to state education boards to put "creation science"—an oxymoron if ever there was one—in the biology textbooks went into making sure that class conflict was kept out of history texts, and race conflict tuned down as much as possible.

As Nash points out, people miss the overarching themes, the secure categories, the grand syntheses, the stories of Great Men. These are the first things to go when generalizations about history are exploded by close attention to gender, ethnic and class difference. Narrative history, *pace* some theorists, number-crunchers and cliometricians, is by no means dead. It still commands an enormous audience, and is perhaps the only kind of history that will ever be truly popular. But the narratives are in change, and even if we wanted to, we cannot will ourselves back to a time when such changes had not yet occurred. I remember watching Kenneth Clark explaining the Renaissance in *Civilization,* twenty years ago. There he stood, in his imperturbable tweeds, against a background of vineyards near Urbino. He had just quoted Yeats's lines on Guidobaldo di Montefeltro, who

> when he made
> That mirror-school of courtesies
> Upon Urbino's windy hill,
> Had sent no runners to and fro
> That he might learn the shepherds' will.

Quite so, said Clark; but "What about the people in the fields, or those shepherds whom Mr. Yeats rightly supposed that Guidobaldo did not consult on matters of taste and good manners? Could they not have had a civilization of their own?" The thought came and went: perhaps now, four hours into the thirteen-hour series, we will hear some acknowledgment that the lower classes had at least done *something* to create the material wealth on which the court of Urbino—and "civilization" in general—rose. But no; their achievement was to have created another work of art, the Tuscan landscape, whose function was to fill onlookers like Clark and us with "the impression of timeless order." It is fairly safe to say that nobody, in the foreseeable future, is likely to discuss the relations between labor and culture in such terms on television, or perhaps anywhere else; and I don't see that as much of a loss.

Broadly speaking, what has happened in the rewriting of

histories has its analogue in American literature departments. There, the arrival of the "New Critics" was greeted with horror by the entrenched remainder of the old guard of "humanists"—wouldn't these close, cold-hearted textual readings destroy the ennobling penumbra of the works of Shelley, Dryden, Shakespeare? Then the new guard became the old, and saw in the arrival of French poststructuralism the wholesale "politicization" of literary studies. And yet, every time, the extremities are drawn back and absorbed into the center.

So it is with the range of historical studies. Academic historians once felt threatened, even insulted, by the idea of "history from below." One of the most interesting and vivacious books to come my way recently was *Journal of My Life,* written by an 18th-century French glazier named Jacques-Louis Ménétra, which had lain buried in manuscript form for two centuries until its publication in 1986. Though I am certainly no specialist in the social history of 18th-century Paris, I felt while reading it as though I was passing over a reef in a glass-bottomed boat, seeing unfamiliar forms with stereoscopic clarity: Ménétra's omnivorous, bawdy, immensely revealing account of his life as "a man of the people" is a proletarian counterpart to Rousseau's *Confessions*; it is also full of self-aggrandizing fantasy and make-believe, but, as Robert Darnton remarked in his Introduction, this too "gives us a chance to see what eighteenth-century dreams were made of." Fifty years ago, very few formal historians in America would have thought it worth much, since its author was not an important figure and did not influence large events. I vividly remember coming across a somewhat similar text in the archives of the Mitchell Library in Sydney, the unread, untranscribed journal of a convict named Laurence Frayne, which turned out to be an incomparable window into the realities of the punishment system on Norfolk Island by one who had suffered them to the full; on its envelope some past archivist's hand had written in pencil "Convict journal— nothing of interest." The initial reaction to the emergence of women's studies, black studies, gay and other minority studies, and their subsequent spread through the once-settled categories of the study of American history, was the same: first, a denial that these groups needed histories of their own, then a succession of adventurous works showing that they did and do, and then a gradual absorption of them to the point where they take their place in the mainstream curriculum. With, all along the way, various Jeremiahs pointing out that the whole trend has gone too far.

By the same token, great changes have taken place in the versions of American history taught to schoolchildren. No serious educator doubts that these were needed, and still are; and it still comes as a shock to read what has been given out as history in the past. Here is a passage from a fifth-grade textbook, dealing with slavery.

> Back of the big house stand rows of small cabins. In these cabins live the families of Negro slaves. . . . The small black boys and girls are pleased to have the white children come to play with them. . . . In time many people came to think that it was wrong to own slaves. Some of the people who owned slaves became angry at this. They said that the black people were better off as slaves in America than they would have been as wild savages in Africa. Perhaps this was true. Most of the slaves seemed happy and contented.

This disgusting pastorale comes from a textbook called *My Country,* published by the state of California and used in its schools in the 1950s. It is inconceivable that such stuff could get into an American textbook today. The last ten years have brought enormous and hard-won gains in accuracy, proportion and sensitivity in the textbook treatment of American minorities, whether Asian, native, black or Hispanic.

But this is not enough for some extremists, who take the view that only blacks can write the history of slavery, only native Indians that of pre-European America, and so forth. They are proposing, not an informed multiculturalism, but a blinkered and wildly polemical separatism. This separatism, in the main, is what conservatives attack *as* "multiculturalism." What is more, the purveyors of this separatist history—based, as the New York State Board of Regents coyly put it, on "non-canonical knowledge and techniques" and "non-dominant knowledge sources," meaning for the most part legend, hearsay and fantasy—want to make sure that it is not just taught at universities, where at least it can be effectively debated, but thrust into the secondary school curriculum as well, where it can't.

That is the object of a bizarre document called the Portland African-American Baseline Essays, which has never been published as a book but, in Xerox form, is altering the curricula of school systems all over the country.[8] Written by an undistinguished group of black scholars and academic wannabes, these essays on history, social studies, math, language arts and science are meant to be a charter of Afrocentrist history for young black Americans. They have had little scrutiny in the mainstream press. But they are popular with bureaucrats like Thomas Sobol, the education commissioner in New York State—people who are scared of alienating black voters or can't stand up to pseudo-scholars like Leonard Jefferies. Their implications for American education are large, and mostly bad. We therefore need to know what they say.

VI

You can summarize the Afrocentrist claim quite easily. It says that the history of the cultural relations between Africa and Europe is bunk—a prop for the fiction of white European supremacy. Palaeohistorians generally agree that intelligent human life began in the Rift Valley of Africa. The Afrocentrist goes further: the African was the *cultural* father of us all. European culture derives from Egypt, and Egypt is part of Africa, linked to its heart by the artery of the Nile. Egyptian civilization begins in sub-Saharan Africa, in Ethiopia and the Sudan.

Hence, argued the founding father of Afrocentrist history, the late Senegalese writer Cheikh Anta Diop, whatever is Egyptian is African, part of the lost black achievement; Imhotep, the genius who invented the pyramid as a monumental form in the 3rd millennium B.C., was black, and so were Euclid and Cleopatra in Alexandria twenty dynasties later.[9] Blacks in Egypt invented hieroglyphics, and monumental stone sculpture, and the pillared temple, and the cult of the Pharaonic sun-king. The Afrocentrist does not mean this as a cultural metaphor of a racially mixed society, designed to call attention to the wide spectrum of skin pigment that existed, as we know, in ancient Egypt. He means that the Egyptians were *black,* with dark skin, long limbs and woolly hair: an observation supported by one ambiguous remark by the Greek historian Herodotus, who visited Egypt in the 5th century B.C., and by not much else. And so the habit of European and American historians of treating the ancient Egyptians as other than black is a racist plot to conceal the achievements of black Africa.

Now it is a fact, documented at length by Martin Bernal in his controversial book *Black Athena,* that writers both popular and academic in the 19th and 20th centuries sought to portray the Egyptians as "whiter" than they can possibly have been—James Breasted, doyen of archaeological studies at the University of Chicago, used to claim in the 1930s that the Egyptians were "dark-skinned members of the Great White Race," and Hollywood agreed. Cleopatra may not have been as black as Bessie Smith, as Afrocentrists claim, but she certainly didn't look like the present Mrs. Larry Fortensky.

It is equally true that 19th- and earlier 20th-century scholars, in trying to detach Egypt from Africa, were wrong, and that their efforts were motivated by bigotry. Geographically, Egypt is part of Africa; and few historians now seem to favor the skin-saving hypothesis that a "dynastic race" came from outside Africa to create Pharaonic Egypt. As Basil Davidson pointed out, the Egyptian racial mix was certainly added to by Near Eastern migrations, but

> to argue from this that the vast majority of the inhabitants of old Egypt, not being "Negro," were therefore not African is as little tenable as to argue the same about the Berbers and the Ethiopians, whom nobody has yet proposed to erase from the list of African peoples. The old racial categories of "white" and "black" can indeed make little sense in this or perhaps any other connection. . . . Whatever their pigmentation or physical appearance, the Egyptians of Pharaonic times may safely be assigned to African history.[10]

Wrangling about the ethnicity of Egyptians—as if there were a single ethnic constant along the Nile for four millennia—is pointless, since no ancient Egyptian would have attached the same racial, political or geographical meanings to the word "Africa" that we do, and in any case African society seems to have been drawn at least as much from the Mesopotamian and Asian peoples east of the Nile as from the African ones west and south of it. The question of whether the ancient Egyptians were black is unimportant to either Egyptian or African history—it only matters to American Afrocentrists.

Black figures do appear in Egyptian art, but they are usually identified as people from the south. For others, the Egyptian artists—whose frescoes provide a wealth of information about the different colors of old Egyptian society—reserved a range of reddish-browns, creamy whites and ochres; they did not see themselves as black, or represent their figures with negroid features. Probably they would have viewed modern American categories of race as meaninglessly crude. They had a theocratic state, but its ethnic composition was closer to a Benetton ad.

As for Herodotus' views on the blackness of Egyptians, these need to be taken with a grain of salt. Herodotus' work is full of curiosities and fables about national characteristics which are not, in fact, true. For instance, he declared in Book 3 of his *History* that the skulls of Egyptians were thicker than those of Persians, and claimed to have verified this by going over the skeletons left on a battlefield where a Persian army had routed an Egyptian one: the Persian skulls "are so thin that the merest touch from a pebble will pierce them, but those of the Egyptians . . . are so tough that it is hardly possible to break them." This, he explained, was because the Persians wore skullcaps, whereas the Egyptians from childhood shaved their heads, "so that the bone of the skull is hardened by the action of the sun—this is why they hardly ever go bald, baldness being rarer in Egypt than anywhere else."

But to the Afrocentrists, black Egypt is not a historical guess: it is an article of faith, the key to a system of remedial belief. Cheikh Diop thought that

A look towards the Egypt of antiquity is the best way to conceive and build our cultural future. . . . Egypt is the distant mother of Western cultures and sciences, [and] most of the ideas that we call foreign are often nothing but mixed up . . . images of the creations of our African ancestors, such as Judaism, Christianity, Islam, dialectics . . . arithmetic, geometry, mechanical engineering, astronomy, the novel, poetry, the drama, architecture and the arts.[11]

It's not clear what Diop meant, in detail, by the idea that ancient Egypt provides the model of future Africa, since it was a slave state run by absolute Pharaohs and their priests. I am mystified by his reference to Afro-Egyptian "dialectics"; were the ideological ancestors of Hegel and Marx really loose among the colonnades of Thebes? Angrily denouncing the papyrus Canon? Complaining about the lack of gay and female Sphinx-carvers? On this point, alas, the hieroglyphs are mute.

Diop wanted us to believe nothing can be imported to Africa, nothing is foreign to it, because everything was there already. Basically, and no matter how much his ideas excite some black Americans, Diop was a crank; this kind of naive diffusionism, in which ideas and cultural forms start at point A and then radiate to other cultures, in which all the threads run back to a single cause or center or puppeteer, is not one that finds much favor with historians today, because it ignores the way in which similar ideas and forms are spontaneously born in very widely separated societies. As John Baines, the Professor of Egyptology at Oxford, remarked when reviewing both Diop's and Bernal's books in the *New York Times,* "Not everyone who doubts the tenets of diffusionism is a Eurocentrist. Indeed, diffusionism was itself the product of a racist and colonialist era, and served an ideology of dominance . . . in order to attack the mistaken view that Africans were not autonomous and inventive, [the authors] imply that other cultures could not have been autonomous and inventive."

But Diop's drift is clear enough. Africa can take anything it wants from Euro-American culture and technology without losing its African essence, because everything that is, was in Africa once. It is merely recapturing its stolen property. One might call this the cargo-cult theory of history; it connects to the myth of the Golden Age, when all things were freely available in abundance. The cargo-cult religion is deeply involved with New Guinea nationalism. Its adherents hold that at one time all the "cargo" (material goods) in the world was owned by the New Guineans. Then came the fall of man: the white colonists came and took it away. But soon a Messiah will arrive and give all the cargo, from tinned sardines to Yamaha outboards, back to the New Guineans whose rightful property it is. This will annul the anguish of colonialism. Christians have a similar myth, that of a prelapsarian Paradise and the coming Millennium. Such myths have a social use. They comfort the persecuted and the marginalized—early Christians, colonized New Guineans, and blacks both in America and in Africa who know that their ancient past has been written out of history.

And it was. On this fact, the Afrocentrists are right, although every reputable scholar of black history has dealt with it too. The racism of traditional 19th- and early 20th-century historians when dealing with the cultures of Africa has been appalling. Most of them refused to believe that African societies had a history that was worth telling or even looking for. The catalogue of quotations could go on forever, and one will do for all—Arnold Toynbee, in *A Study of History*: "When we classify mankind by color, the only one of the primary races . . . which has not made a single creative contribution to any of our 21 civilizations is the black race."

No black person—indeed, no modern historian of any race—could read such bland dismissals without incredulity and disgust. The question is: How to correct the record? Only by more knowledge. Toynbee was writing more than fifty years ago, but in the last twenty years, immense strides have been made in the historical scholarship both of Africa and of African America. But the upwelling of research, the growth of Black Studies programs in American universities, and all that goes with the long-needed expansion of the field seems fated to be plagued by movements like Afrocentrism, just as there are always cranks nattering about flying saucers on the edges of meso-American archaeology.

The second claim of Afrocentrism, then, is that European culture owes its very existence to Africa. Africa colonized Europe benignly, by imparting its knowledge to it.

This happened through Egyptian influence on Greece, but in the process the pioneering achievements of Africa were lost or disguised. To plough through the literature of Afrocentrism is to enter a world of claims about technological innovation so absurd that they lie beyond satire, like those made for Russian science in Stalin's time. Egyptians, alias Africans, invented the wet-cell battery by observing electric eels in the Nile. The Afrocentrist "scholar" Ivan van Sertima claims that black Egyptians late in the first millennium B.C. flew around in gliders; this news is based, not on the discovery of an aircraft in an Egyptian tomb, but on a silhouette wooden votive sculpture of the god Horus, a falcon, that a passing English businessman mistook some decades ago for a model airplane. Sertima also teaches that Tanzanians fifteen hundred years ago were smelting steel with semiconductor technology. Like the Afrocentrist historian John Henrik Clarke, he thinks South America was populated by expeditions from Africa whose records have, naturally, been lost; the evidence for this is the thick lips on Olmec sculpture. Likewise, Afrocentrists think the face of the Great Sphinx of Gizeh was actually that of a black, and that Napoleon's soldiers were ordered to mutilate it with cannon-fire to conceal the fact. There is nothing to prove these tales, but nothing to disprove them either— a common condition of things that didn't happen. This kind of bilge is what the members of the New York State Board of Regents mean by "nondominant knowledge sources."

Why do Americans show such gullibility before people with degrees? John Henrik Clarke has a doctorate and is regarded by many blacks as, in Henry Louis Gates Jr.'s words, "the great paterfamilias of the Afrocentric movement." He is also an anti-Semitic crank, given to denouncing what he calls "the Jewish educational mafia"; he penned an Introduction to a racist piece of pseudo-science called *The Iceman Inheritance: Prehistoric Sources of Western Man's Racism, Sexism and Aggression,* whose author, Michael Bradley, argues that Jews are the worst people on earth because they were once the " 'purest' and oldest Neanderthal-Caucasoids." It seems barely credible that American Jews, who were at the forefront of the struggle for civil rights for African-Americans in the 1960s, should now be the targets of anti-Semitic attacks by a new generation of blacks, gulled by teachers like Leonard Jefferies into believing in the historicity of hate-texts like that durable Czarist forgery, the Protocols of the Elders of Zion. But thanks to the rise of Afrocentrist pseudo-scholarship, blacks are the only Americans among whom anti-Semitism, slowly waning elsewhere, is actually on the rise.[12]

This new effusion of racism comes garnished with arguments proposing that, since only those in power can be racists, black racism is not racism at all. And on top of it young blacks are offered the delusory promise of Back-to-Africa sentiment. All American migrant groups draw cultural identity, and a measure of spiritual strength, from a sense of their original roots—in Sicily or the Ionian Islands, in Ireland or Cuba, and in Africa. In longing for the womb they also sentimentalize and stereotype their origins; this, as any outsider who has attended a full-blast Irish beano in Boston can testify, is a powerful tribal instinct. But it ought to be recognized that the "Africa," the imagined entity of which Afrocentrists like to speak, is very largely a construction of this kind—a lost maternal paradise.

American blacks, no less than whites, belong to and are shaped by American culture, to which they have so immensely contributed and into which their own imaginations and deeds are inextricably wound: all they have in common with African blacks is their genes and, in the case of African states that were once English colonies, the English language. To imagine that the cultural experience of an American black resembles that of a citizen of Zimbabwe or Uganda or South Africa, beyond the basic fact that both have suffered the corrosive and demeaning effects of white racism, is fanciful.

In the past there was never, in the strict sense, a pan-African culture: instead, there were many tribes, many languages, many cultures, many contradictory religions and cults, and many kings; and, needless to add, many wars between them. The horrors of post-colonial Africa are largely due to the fact that new black rulers were able to graft modern techniques of oppression onto ancient tribal hatreds; the borders of African nation-states rarely correspond to tribal divisions, so that tribes within a state are often at one another's throats. Fifteen years ago it was already clear that the more benign legacies of British colonialism, such as independent courts and relatively uncorrupted civil services, were among the first things to be dropped by the former British colonies in Africa that turned into nationalist military dictatorships. Who would seriously argue that the Ugandans were worse off, economically or legally, under Lord Lugard in the 1910s than they are now, after Idi Amin and his successors? Zaire, formerly the Belgian Congo, is a bankrupt dystopia whose tyrant, President Mobutu, has about six billion dollars in Switzerland— the national debt of his country. People have been dying of hunger for hundreds of years in Ethiopia, but not until the dictator Mengistu took charge was the mass murder by starvation of millions of people actually used there for political ends. The behavior of French colonial satraps in Guinea was appalling enough, but hardly worse than the corruption and cruelty of Seiko Toure, the black Caligula who took over when the French quit and ran the country from the mid-60s to the early 70s. Moreover, it may be that those African states which had no significant record of European colonization—

Liberia, which was actually founded by American slaves returned to Africa in the 19th century, and Ethiopia—are the ones that turned out worst. The idea that African-Americans have a place waiting for them in some generalized "Africa," in any but a vaguely metaphorical sense, is mere cultural demagogy. Neither black nor white can "go home again," except as tourists; their mutual home, with all its ideals, opportunities, conflicts and evils, is America, and they have no other.

VII

Nowhere are the weakness and propagandistic nature of Afrocentrism more visible than in its version of slave history.

Slavery is one of the oldest and worst of human institutions. Its legacies are with America still, in the suffering and social damage inflicted on its black people, in the racism of its whites. Every kind of rationalization and excuse for this Original Sin of the American republic has in the past suffused the teaching of American history. As Arthur Schlesinger, Jr., among others, has pointed out, American history was long written by and for whites, who usurped the images of Afro-American life and fed them back as distorted stereotypes, consoling to white prejudices and demeaning to black self-knowledge. No general American history written by a white up to the 1960s can be trusted to give a fair, investigatory view of what slavery and its results meant to black Americans—or, by the same token, of what the conquest of the West meant to American Indians. Modern historians, black and white, have labored to set this right. But there is no evil so great that it cannot be exaggerated; and this has become the project of recent Afrocentrists, who wish to invent a sort of remedial history in which the entire blame for the invention and practice of black slavery is laid at the door of Europeans. This is profoundly unhistorical, but it's getting locked in popular consciousness through the new curricula.

There have been three major slave revolts in human history. The first, led by the Thracian gladiator Spartacus against the Romans, occurred in 73 B.C. The third was in the 1790s when the great black revolutionary Toussaint L'Ouverture and his slave army wrested control of Santo Domingo from the French, only to be defeated by Napoleon in 1802. But the second fell halfway between these two, in the middle of the 9th century A.D., and is less documented than either. We do know that the insurgents were black; that the Muslim 'Abbasid caliphs of Iraq had brought them from East Africa to work, in the thousands, in the salt marshes of the delta of the Tigris. These rebels beat back the Arabs for nearly ten years. Like the escaped maroons in Brazil centuries later, they set up their own strongholds in the marshland. They seemed unconquerable and they were not, in fact, crushed by the Muslims until 883. They were known as the Zanj, and they bequeathed their name to the island of Zanzibar in East Africa—which, by no coincidence, would become and remain the market center for slaves in the Arab world until the last quarter of the 19th century.

The revolt of the Zanj eleven hundred years ago should remind us of the utter falsity of the now fashionable line of argument which tries to suggest that the enslavement of African blacks was the invention of European whites. It is true that slavery had been written into the basis of the classical world; Periclean Athens was a slave state, and so was Augustan Rome. Most of their slaves were Caucasian whites, and "In antiquity, bondage had nothing to do with physiognomy or skin color."[13] The word "slave" meant a person of Slavic origin. By the 13th century it spread to other Caucasian peoples subjugated by armies from central Asia: Russians, Georgians, Circassians, Albanians, Armenians, all of whom found ready buyers from Venice to Sicily to Barcelona, and throughout the Muslim world.

But the *African* slave trade as such, the black traffic, was a Muslim invention, developed by Arab traders with the enthusiastic collaboration of black African ones, institutionalized with the most unrelenting brutality centuries before the white man appeared on the African continent, and continuing long after the slave market in North America was finally crushed.

Historically, this traffic between the Mediterranean and sub-Saharan Africa begins with the very civilization that Afrocentrists are so anxious to claim as black—ancient Egypt. African slavery was well in force long before that: but by the first millennium B.C. Pharaoh Rameses II boasts of providing the temples with more than 100,000 slaves, and indeed it is inconceivable that the monumental culture of Egypt could have been raised outside a slave economy. For the next two thousand years the basic economies of sub-Saharan Africa would be tied into the catching, use and sale of slaves. The sculptures of medieval life show slaves bound and gagged for sacrifice, and the first Portuguese explorers of Africa around 1480 found a large slave trade set up from the Congo to Benin. There were large slave plantations in the Mali empire in the 13th-14th centuries and every abuse and cruelty visited on slaves in the antebellum South, including the practice of breeding children for sale like cattle, was practiced by the black rulers of those towns which the Afrocentrists now hold up as sanitized examples of high civilization, such as Timbuktu and Songhay.

Naturally this is a problem for Afrocentrists, especially in the context of the black Muslim ideas that many of them espouse. Nothing in the writings of the Prophet forbids slavery, which is why it became such an Arab-dominated business. A big lie is needed to neutralize this inconvenient truth. Consequently one of the best-sellers in the American black community at present is an official publication of the group known as The Nation of Islam (whose head is the arch-bigot Louis Farrakhan), entitled *The Secret Relationship Between Blacks and Jews,* a compilation of pseudo-history which pretends to disclose the "inordinate" role played by Jews in creating "slavery and the black holocaust." Its allegations—such as the fiction that Jewish merchants "frequently dominated" the slave trade to America and the Caribbean—have been painstakingly refuted, point by point, in a response by the historian Harold Brackman, often using the very sources misused and misquoted by Farrakhan's version of history. Yet his reply could not penetrate the black community as *The Secret Relationship* has done, since it is in the nature of paranoid texts to inoculate naive readers against their rebuttal; any reply becomes part of the huge global conspiracy itself.[14]

In the Baseline Essays and elsewhere, one gets a flat denial that Egypt had slaves at all, which would have been news to Moses, and a lot of mumbling about how African slavery, well, existed, sort of, but was more benign than its American counterpart. But there are no generalizations to be made about this; sometimes the African slaves of Africans seem to have been accepted almost as family or tribal members, though with very diminished rights, and sometimes they were treated as something less than cattle, beaten and raped and starved—again, an archetypal pattern which would be repeated by white slaveowners in the old South. As Roland Oliver, the most distinguished of African scholars and the general editor of the eight-volume Cambridge History of Africa, has shown: All that we know of the slave traffic as it expanded between the 16th and 19th centuries confirms that it could not have existed without the wholehearted cooperation of African tribal states, built on the supply of captives generated by their relentless wars.[15]

The image promulgated by pop-history fictions like *Roots*—white slavers bursting with cutlass and musket into the settled lives of peaceful African villages—is very far from the historical truth. A marketing system had been in place for centuries, and its supply was controlled by Africans.

Nor did it simply vanish with Abolition.

In 1865, the year the Civil War ended in the defeat of the South, Livingstone was in Zanzibar; he estimated that between 80,000 and 100,000 African slaves were brought down in chains from the interior by Arab and African slavers that year, loaded on the dhows and shipped off to Persia and the Arabian Gulf states.

Unlike the English and the Americans, neither the Arabs nor the African kings in the 19th century saw the smallest humanitarian reason to move against slavery. Slave markets, supplying the Arab emirates, were still operating in Djibouti in the 1950s; and since 1960, the slave trade has flourished in Mauritania and the Sudan. There are still reports of chattel slavery in northern Nigeria, Rwanda and Niger. Jean-Bedel

Bokassa, emperor of the Central African Republic, whom a diamond-hungry Giscard d'Estaing ostentatiously embraced as his black brother at the time of his coronation in 1977, kept hundreds of slaves and from time to time arranged a massacre of them for his own amusement. If, as H. Rap Brown once observed, violence is as American as apple pie, then slavery would seem to be as African as yams.

And yet the idea of the solitary guilt of Europe and America continues to haunt discussions of slavery. Some African and even American black leaders, including—rather surprisingly—the Rev. Jesse Jackson, have actually proposed that America and the developed industrial nations of Europe, which profited from slavery, should now contribute a form of blood-money to African states as official reparation for the social and economic damage done to the continent in the past by the slave trade, so as to help these states build up their economic base. Modern Africa, they argue, has as much right to this as Israel had to the immense subventions that have been paid to it by America and other countries as penance for Hitler's murder of European Jews. Curiously, none of them suggest that the Arab emirates or Iraq should kick in their share, which, by all rights, should be a very large one, larger than Europe's or even America's, and just as easily raised from the flow of oil. If Washington must pay cash for the sins of Simon Legree, then it seems only fair that Baghdad should expiate those of the 'Abassid caliphs.

Africa, Islam and Europe all participated in black slavery, enforced it, profited from its miseries. But in the end, only Europe (including, here, North America) proved itself able to conceive of abolishing it; only the immense moral and intellectual force of the Enlightenment, brought to bear on

the hideous oppression that slavery represented, was able—
unevenly and with great difficulty—to bring the trade to an
end. That we now have so-called historians who are prepared
to gloss over this fact strikes me as remarkable. But then, in
these latitudes, neither Occam's Razor nor the notion that the
burden of proof rests on the person making the assertion has
any force.

For here we come up against a cardinal rule of the PC
attitude to oppression studies. Whatever a white European
male historian or witness has to say must be suspect; the
utterances of an oppressed person or group deserve instant
credence, even if they're the merest assertion. Now the claims
of the victim do have to be heard, because they may cast new
light on history. But they have to pass exactly the same tests
as anyone else's, or debate fails and truth suffers. The PC
cover for this is the idea that all statements about history are
expressions of power: history is only written by the winners
and truth is political and unknowable, unless some victim
knows it in his or her bones.

This sophistry is what enables the authors of the Portland
African-American Baseline Essays not only to sow the curriculum with fictions about Egyptian science, but to insert the
most ludicrous nonsense about science itself by equating it
with magic. Thus we learn that the all-black Egyptians, when
they were not flitting about in gliders, could foretell the future
with "astropsychological treatises." They could see things that
were out of sight, or before they happened. They got the
pyramids built by telekinesis—concentrate hard enough, and
you can make a hundred-ton block of limestone float in the
air. At least this Shirley MacLaine-style archaeology disposes
of the awkward problem of Egyptian slave labor, since we

wouldn't want those black Egyptians to have slaves themselves. The essay from which we learn all this, and much else, is written by Hunter Havelin Adams III, who describes himself as a "Research Scientist at Argonne National Laboratories, Chicago." This sounds vaguely impressive but in fact, according to Argonne, Mr. Adams is a lab assistant whose task is to collect air samples, with no qualifications beyond a high-school diploma. Another remedial exercise, this time in biography.

VIII

The word "self-esteem" has become one of the obstructive shibboleths of education. Why do black children need Afrocentrist education? Because, its promoters say, it will create self-esteem. They live in a world of media and institutions whose images and values are mainly created by whites. The white tradition is to denigrate blacks. Hence blacks must have models that show them that they are different, and that they matter. Do you want your children to love themselves? Then change the curriculum. Feed them racist claptrap about how your intelligence is a function of the amount of melanin in your skin, and how Africans were sun people, free and open and cooperative, whereas Europeans were ice people, skulking pallidly in caves.

The self-esteem talk comes to us wrapped in sentiments which, if uttered by whites, would set off alarm-bells of racism. Black children, one reads in the Portland Baseline Essays, are impelled by their genetic heritage to "process information

differently" from white ones—a claim which white suprema-
cists, from their side of the fence, have been making since
before the Civil War. The fact is that, to quote Albert Shanker,
the president of the American Federation of Teachers, "poor,
minority children, whose performance still lags far behind
that of white, middle-class kids, deserve the best education
we can give them. They're not going to get it if we substitute
myths for history or magic for science."

Out of this farrago the Afrocentrists want to create a separatist history and impose it on kids who are still too young
to dispute it. There is even talk of curricular change along the
Portland lines for three-year-olds. It is not hard to see why
these claims for purely remedial history are intensifying today.
They are symbolic. They are part of a reaction of despair,
frustration and rage against twelve years of rightwing government, the stubbornly anti-reform policies of Reagan and
Bush, the Republicans' assimilation of racism with populism.
By 1989 about 44 percent of all black children lived below
the poverty line, while the hopes for racial equality and greater
educational opportunity for impoverished African-Americans
that had been raised in the mid-60s were all but extinct.

But that only makes the claims for Afrocentrist pseudo-
history understandable. It does not justify it, or lend it credence as knowledge. Nationalism always wants to have myths
to prop itself up; and the newer the nationalism, the newer
the myth, the more ancient its claims.

That was how Irish cultural nationalists—Yeats and his
friends in the 1890s—were able to create a mythic past for
Ireland, the Celtic twilight full of heroes and lost kings, Cu-
chulain and Briann Boru. It is why the tartan, unknown in
ancient Scotland, was actually the invention of late 18th- and

19th-century textile manufacturers. It is why the Catalans in the 19th century, bitterly resenting the suppression of their language and the loss of their political autonomy to Madrid after the conquest of Barcelona by the Bourbons in 1714, created an entire system of cultural revival based on a highly selective, and mythologized, version of their own medieval past and its lost institutions. The invention of tradition, as Eric Hobsbawm and others have shown in detail,[16] was one of the cultural industries of 19th-century Europe.

And of the 20th century too. And if you ask what the aim of these efforts to roll history and myth together was, in every case the answer is the same. Self-esteem. The Germans suffered from low self-esteem after the Treaty of Versailles. The Italians had low self-esteem in the 20s, and were understandably tired of being viewed as a nation of organ-grinders and gelato-makers. Irish self-esteem had been debased by seven hundred years of English colonization and religious prejudice, by the disenfranchisement of the Catholics. But the desire for self-esteem does not justify every lie and exaggeration and therapeutic slanting of evidence that can be claimed to alleviate it. The separatism it fosters turns what ought to be a recognition of cultural diversity, of real multiculturalism, generous and tolerant on both sides, into a pernicious symbolic program. Separatism is the opposite of diversity, and it can also make unholy alliances. Nearly thirty years ago Malcolm X's Black Muslims and George Lincoln Rockwell's American Nazi Party staged a joint rally at Madison Square Garden to dramatize their mutual hope of splitting the United States into segregated zones, one for blacks, the other for whites.

The idea that European culture is oppressive, in and of

itself, is a fallacy that can only survive among the fanatical and the ignorant. The moral and intellectual conviction that inspired Toussaint L'Ouverture to focus the grievances of the Haitian slaves and lead them to freedom came from his reading of Rousseau and Mirabeau. When thousands of voteless, propertyless workers the length and breadth of England met in their reading-groups in the 1820s to discuss republican ideas and discover the significance of Shakespeare's *Julius Caesar,* they were seeking to unite themselves by taking back the meanings of a dominant culture from custodians who didn't live up to them. For the last two hundred years, the victims of oppression have always been able to find a transforming and strengthening vision within the literature and thought of Europe. It is an act of the shoddiest condescension to suppose that this can no longer be so, and that this immense, complicated, many-celled edifice, this beehive that reductionists mistake for a "monolith," can no longer contain any answers to the needs of the weak, the aspirations of the deprived and the demands of those who seek cultural self-definition.

American ideas of liberal democracy are only to be nourished at their sources, which lie absolutely within the European tradition; and it is far more important that the young should know about them before they go on to acquire whatever acquaintance they may wish to have with the ancient culture of the Dogon or the political institutions of the Iroquois. First things first. Cultural separatism within this republic is more a fad than a serious proposal; it is not likely to hold, but if it did, it would be an educational disaster for those it claims to help, the young, the poor and the black. It would be a gesture not of "empowerment," but of emasculation. Self-esteem comes from doing things well, from discovering how to tell a truth from a lie, and from finding out what unites us as well as what separates us. The posturing of the politically correct, and their guilt-ridden tolerance for con-men like Leonard Jefferies and the Rev. Al Sharpton, is no more a guide to such matters than the opinions of Simon Legree.

LECTURE 3

Moral in Itself: Art and the Therapeutic Fallacy

*I*N MATTERS OF VISUAL ART, the American "culture war" officially started on May 18, 1989, on the floor of the U.S. Senate in Washington, when Senator Alfonse D'Amato (Republican, N.Y.) tore up a reproduction of a photograph and threw the pieces on the floor. He had been sent it by the Rev. Donald Wildmon, a religious activist whose pressure-group, the American Family Association, had been formed to combat the spread of pornography, indecency and irreligious sentiment in America. Wildmon's specialty is finding bad messages, overt and subliminal, in media and the arts, and then bringing write-in pressure to bear on sponsor companies. In the past he had campaigned against such things as David Wolper's TV adaptation of Colleen McCullough's best-selling religious weepie *The Thorn Birds,* Martin Scorsese's film *The Last Temptation of Christ* and Madonna's music videos. He managed to pressure CBS into removing a 3.5-second sequence from a Ralph Bakshi cartoon in which Mighty Mouse was shown sniffing a flower: what the devious rodent was *really* sniffing, Wildmon insisted, was cocaine.[1]

The image reproduced a photograph by an artist, Andres Serrano. It showed a cheap plastic crucifix, of the kind sold everywhere in devotional stores and religious-kitsch shops, submerged in an amber-colored fluid streaked with bubbles. The title of the artwork, *Piss Christ*, made it clear what the liquid was. It was the artist's own. *Piss Christ* was in every way an autograph work.

If Serrano had called his large and technically splendid Cibachrome print something else—*La Catedral Ahogada*, perhaps, or more prosaically *Immersion Study* (*I*)—there would have been no way of knowing that it was pee. But Serrano wanted to make a sharp, jolting point about two things: first, the degradation of mass religious imagery into kitsch (inescapable in America, as any thoughtful Christian is aware), and second, his resentment of the coercive morality of his own Hispanic-Catholic roots. Serrano is a highly conflicted lapsed Catholic, and his work—particularly images like *Piss Christ*—is about those conflicts. No image is without a history, and Serrano's is a fairly old strain in modern art—Surrealist anticlerical blasphemy. *Piss Christ* has a number of remote ancestors, including Max Ernst's famous/infamous painting of the Virgin Mary spanking the Infant Jesus and the blurred photo, ancestor of the modern "happening," of a Surrealist poet cussing out a priest on a Paris sidewalk in the 1920s.

Not all of Serrano's work seeks its effects through blasphemy. But *Piss Christ* certainly did, and there was no way around it.

Of course, after the event, you can historicize and demur all you like. You can point out that the plastic crucifixion wasn't actually Christ, but a *representation* of Christ—but this Magrittean sophistry, *ceci n'est pas un Dieu,* doesn't work. The image is too strong.

You can also remark that crucifixes are commercially produced for all sorts of weird reasons, without causing moral storms: thus in the same month that the politicians began to do their stuff over Serrano, I received a catalogue from a mail-order cutlery firm, specializing in hunting and fishing knives, which advertised a little weapon worthy in conception, if not in craftsmanship, of the Borgias: a stiletto concealed in a crucifix, made in Taiwan, and selling for $15.99. This, one might think, was not without its blasphemous aspect too. And last Easter, the local drugstore in the part of eastern Long Island where I live was selling chocolate crucifixes with a vague lumpish figure of Jesus molded into them: "Eat this in memory of Me." Why it should be OK for some Americans to eat an image of their Saviour and turn it into feces, while other Americans were convulsed at the idea of taking another image of the same Saviour and dunking it in urine, seemed a riddle fit to stop a modern Tocqueville in his tracks. But not in the American heartland, where the religion industry is immune to criticism or doubt.

However, neither the stiletto-crucifix nor the chocolate Jesus had been rewarded with money that came from the U.S. government, and the author of *Piss Christ* had been. Shortly before Donald Wildmon sent his complaint to Senator D'Amato, Serrano had received a prize of $15,000 from the South-Eastern Center for Contemporary Art (SECCA) in Winston-Salem. SECCA had received the money for this award—before its jury decided to give it to Serrano—from the National Endowment for the Arts (NEA). It came without strings, and nobody in the NEA had the least role in choosing Serrano as winner. Nevertheless, Serrano had indirectly wound up with government money, a situation which Wildmon declared in a circular letter to mean that "the bias and bigotry against Christians, which has dominated television and movies for the past decade or more, has now moved over to the art museums," and that it presaged an era of "physical persecution of Christians"—if not by feeding them to the lions of the Colosseum as in Roman antiquity, then maybe by flinging them to sharks circling in huge tubs of urine in SeaWorld. Thus cued by Wildmon, Senator D'Amato rose in the Senate to denounce the NEA. "This is an outrage, and our people's tax dollars should not support this trash, and we should not be giving it the dignity." He then read into the record a letter signed by some two dozen (mostly conservative Republican) senators, protesting that the work "is shocking, abhorrent, and completely underserving of any recognition whatsoever. Millions of taxpayers are rightfully incensed. . . . There is a clear flaw in the procedures used to select art and artists deserving of the taxpayers' support. . . . This matter does not involve freedom of artistic expression."

But it did; and the proof of that unfolded during the scandal that next arose over the work of the photographer Robert Mapplethorpe.

To me, the interest of the Mapplethorpe affair lies in its stark display of colliding American values—but not much else. Despite the enthusiasm of his fans, I have never been able to think of him as a major photographer. I first visited his New York studio in 1970; at the time his work, such as it was, consisted of fetishistic but banal collages of beefcake photos with the addition of things like a leopardskin jockstrap or a gauze patch with a pus-stain on it. "That," I told myself as I was going down the stairs forty minutes later, "is a talent we're not going to hear much about." If you had told me then that Robert Mapplethorpe would be as famous as Jackson Pollock within twenty years, and that the scandal produced by his work would threaten the equilibrium of the whole relationship between museums and government in America, I would have said you were crazy. So much for the critic as forecaster.

I saw quite a lot of his work, though not of Mapplethorpe himself, over the ensuing years: the heavy, brutal S&M images of the X portfolio, the elegant overpresented photos of Lisa Lyons, the icy male nudes in homage to Horst and Baron von Gloeden, the Edward Weston flowers. It was the work of a man who knew the history of photographs, for whom the camera was an instrument of quotation. As Mike Weaver, editor of the forthcoming Oxford *History of Photography,* pointed out to me much later, "his best work . . . is the group of somewhat formalist, indeed geometric, nudes based on an 1890s' taste for ritual magic of the kind expressed earlier by another great gay photographer, Fred Holland Day. [His] use of the pentangle in human form comes from his mock-Satanic commitment to the inverted pentagram of Eliphas Lévi, master of Aleister Crowley . . . Never a Post-Modernist, not even a Modernist, he was a real reactionary. This, of course, is why he is so popular. Like Simeon Solomon and Beardsley before him, Mapplethorpe was a Symbolist with a Mannerist style." One image in particular from the X portfolio confirms this analysis—Mapplethorpe's self-portrait posing as Satan himself, the tail supplied by a bullwhip jammed up his ass, the lash trailing on the floor.

In the X portfolio, the mannered chic of his images was

slammed back into immediacy by the pornographic violence
of his subject-matter. But I don't think chic is a value, and I
felt at odds with the culture of affectless quotation that had
taken over New York art, and my notions of sexual bliss did
not coincide with Mapplethorpe's, and so when he asked me
to write a catalogue introduction to his show—the show that
was to cause all the trouble—I had to tell him that since the
X portfolio was obviously a key to his work and (I thought
at the time) his main claim to originality, and since I found
the images of sexual humiliation and torture in it (fistfucking,
heavy bondage, and a man pissing into another water-
sporter's mouth) too disgusting to write about with enthusiasm, he had better find someone else. Which he did. Several,
in fact.

Now most of us know, at least in outline, what happened
to Mapplethorpe's retrospective in 1988–90, *The Perfect Moment*. It was shown in Pennsylvania and Boston without the
slightest incident, and at the Whitney Museum in New York
to scenes of enthusiasm rivaling the palmiest moments of his
mentor, Andy Warhol. But when the show was about to
appear at the Corcoran Gallery in Washington, it came under
heavy attack from conservatives on the ground that the display
was partially underwritten by a grant from the National Endowment for the Arts, and that the government had no right
to be spending taxpayers' money on supporting work so repugnant to the general moral sensibility of the American
public.

In point of fact the Corcoran had received no NEA funds
to mount the Robert Mapplethorpe show, although it had
received them for other projects in the past. The NEA support
money for Mapplethorpe went to the Institute of Contempo-

rary Art at the University of Pennsylvania, which had curated the exhibition in the first place. The sum involved was $30,000, representing about one-sixtieth of one percent of a copper penny for every man, woman and child in America; but still, as Hilton Kramer and others were at pains to point out, it was public money all the same. There had been no protest, let alone "public outrage," over the display before it headed for Washington. Nevertheless that tribune of the people Senator Jesse Helms saw in Mapplethorpe a golden opportunity to raise right-wing consciousness about obscenity and filth, and when the dewlaps of his wrath started shaking outside the Corcoran, it caved in and canceled the show. Helms and other conservatives, including Senators Alfonse D'Amato and Orrin Hatch, then tried to push an amendment through the Senate, preventing the NEA from underwriting such anti-social stuff again. The Helms amendment proposed that no government funds should be given by the NEA to "promote, disseminate or produce," in its exact words,

(1) obscene or indecent materials, including but not limited to depictions of sadomasochism, homo-eroticism, the exploitation of children, or individuals engaged in sex acts; or

(2) material which denigrates the objects or beliefs of the adherents of a particular religion or non-religion; or,

(3) material which denigrates, debases, or reviles a person, group or class of citizens on the basis of race, creed, sex, handicap, age or national origin.

The most obvious and curious feature of the Helms amendment was that, if it had not issued from a famously right-wing Republican senator, you could have mistaken it—

especially its last two clauses—for any ruling on campus speech limitations recently proposed by the nominally left-wing agitators for political correctness. It was hard to know exactly what Helms meant by "a particular religion or non-religion" but certainly clause (3) made it clear that he was against racism, sexism, ableism, lookism and any of the other offenses against social etiquette whose proscription by PC was already causing such mirth and laughter among the neo-conservatives. Thus extremes meet.

The other peculiarity of the Helms amendment was to be so broadly drafted as to become virtually meaningless. It would, as I pointed out the following week in *Time,* have created a loony parody of cultural democracy in which every citizen became his or her own Cato the Censor. All that a work of art would need to be de-funded, or (if shown in a museum under NEA auspices) removed from view, would be to "offend" anyone for practically any reason at all. The amendment was thus a crystallization of our Culture of Complaint into law. It would have made the NEA hostage to every crank, ideologue and God-botherer in America. A grant for an exhibition of, say, Gothic ivories could be pulled on the grounds that the material was objectionable to Jews (much medieval art is anti-Semitic), to Muslims (what about those scenes of false prophets boiling in hell with Muhammad?), or, for that matter, to atheists offended by the use of government money to insert any sort of religious propaganda, including ancient ivory carvings, into a museum. Some Stalinist feminist could complain that a 13th-century depiction of a patriarchal God, or the sexism implicit in a subservient or tempting Eve, was repugnant to her "religion or non-religion." Under the Helms amendment, a fire-worshipper might even claim that the presence of extinguishers in the museum offended *his* god.

Helms and his supporters were at pains to deny that the amendment had anything to do with censorship. Where could those liberals have got such an idea? Censorship: that meant repressing works of art (or "so-called 'art,' " to use the correct locution) that people made on their own time and with their own money. Refusing government money to "promote" indecency wasn't censorship. Decadents like Mapplethorpe, and blasphemers like Serrano, could do what they wanted with their own time and money. But let them not come skulking and sniffing after that one six-thousandth of one penny of the average decent American's tax dollar. (Generally, the fact that neither Serrano nor Mapplethorpe had applied for, or directly received, any money from the NEA tended to get lost in the rhetoric. None of Mapplethorpe's or Serrano's photos were made with NEA support; all the same, due to the successful propaganda of the religious and political right, millions of Americans still imagine that the NEA came chasing after them both, stuffing dollars down their shirts to help them do their worst.)

Nevertheless, one would have needed to be remarkably naive to think that censorship was *not* the root of the controversy. The efforts to cut off government money from "offensive" art were only the tip of a general effort growing on the right to repress *all* "offensive" art, subsidized or not. The wisest analysis of this problem was offered, some months later, by a Jesuit: the Rev. Timothy Healy, the president of the New York Public Library. "The debate is about censorship," Father Healy declared to a House Subcommittee on Postsecondary Education in November 1989,[2]

and any effort to pretend it is not is misleading. Given the prestige of the Federal Government, the accolade that any grant from either national endowment bestows, and the artistic integrity and impartiality of the juries who work for the endowments, any canons of content-based condemnation are simply a priori restraint. Against the argument that the artist is free to write, to paint or to compose as he pleases without federal subsidy, we must urge that to deprive an artist of that subsidy because of the content of his work is a clear and strong kind of censorship. The counter-argument is really a dodge that does not take into account the realities of the artistic marketplace or, indeed, the rights of the artist himself. . . .

The course of the debate shows a definite confusion between law and morality. . . . Once law and morality are confused it is easy to arrive at such statements as "whatever is good ought to be legislated." That premise is bad enough but the mixing up of the realm of law with the realm of morals, is deadly. . . . Law can tolerate evils that morality condemns. . . . We have a good law if it will be obeyed, if it is enforceable, and if it is so prudently drafted that it avoids most of the harmful effects that could flow from it. If a law does none of these things it is a bad law, no matter what the logic or the moral intensity behind it.

Though none of the arguments heard on the Senate floor attained the clarity and sophistication of this priest's words, the Helms amendment was voted down, by 73 votes to 24. The Senate decided that the definition of pornography should be left to the courts.

And into court it went. The Mapplethorpe show moved on to Cincinnati, where the conservatives decided to make a test case out of it, arraigning the director of the Contemporary Arts Center for public obscenity.

There was much pessimistic hand-wringing in the artworld over what would happen when the X portfolio was shown to a bunch of, well, rubes in the Midwest. But once again a kind of natural American common sense, maybe more common in Cincinnati than in Soho, prevailed. Largely because the prosecution could not find any credible expert witnesses against the work, the director was acquitted and the Mapplethorpe circus rolled on; the dead photographer was by now either a culture-hero or a culture-demon; but either way, everyone from Maine to Albuquerque had heard of him, and the net economic result of Senator Helms's objurgations had been to push the prices of X portfolio prints from about $10,000 to somewhere around $100,000.

But the Mapplethorpe debacle had two broad cultural results. First, it caused paranoia in the relations between American museums and their funding sources. It produced an atmosphere of doubt, self-censorship and disoriented caution among curators and museum directors, when it came to raising money and facing the political demands of pressure groups.

And second, it marked the demise of American aestheticism, and revealed the bankruptcy of the culture of therapeutics which had come to dominate the way so many cultural professionals in this country were apt to argue the relations between art and its public. To argue what I mean I am going to have to leave Mapplethorpe, leave our fin-de-siècle, and circle back to a much earlier time. But the first result needs to be looked at first, in the context of the highly charged—and, for high culture, increasingly toxic—political atmosphere that envelops the relations between government and the arts in America today.

II

By the end of 1991 it was clear that the agenda of American conservatives, depending on their IQ and cultural backgound, was either to destroy the National Endowment for the Arts altogether, or else to restrict its benefactions to purely "mainstream" events. The latter seemed more likely, given political realities: too many rich Republicans (and Democrats too, of course) have a stake in the kind of prestige that cultural good works confer in their home cities—such as support of the local museum or symphony orchestra—to allow the NEA to perish altogether. Nevertheless it was symptomatic of the present panic over state cultural funding that Patrick Buchanan, not so much neo-conservative as neolithic in his cultural views, could have forced George Bush to fire the head of the NEA, John Frohnmayer, in order to appease the know-nothings and fag-bashers on the right of the GOP. The religious right's attacks on this issue are not likely to taper off now that Bill Clinton has replaced George Bush. Indeed, since Clinton is seen by the Bible-thumpers as a demonic liberal, and since religious conservatism has lost so much of its power base in Washington, it is far more likely that the pressures for cultural censorship will increase: it is the easiest of all buttons to press, and the right has been leaning on it too long to ease off now. Attacks on the NEA have become part of the standard background noise of politics by now, just like attacks on the Public Broadcasting System. They are part of an escalating war over cultural issues, and they will not go away.

For the 80s brought a rising conflict over the "ideological ownership" of popular culture in America, an issue to which the content of TV broadcasting is ineluctably bound. Given the present atmosphere of intolerance, one could hardly expect the right—especially the religious right, and those politicians who either are in it or fear its votes—not to wade into this with their hobnails on.

No area of our institutional culture was more vulnerable to this than broadcasting, a favorite target of Republican attack-politics. The mandated independence of the Public Broadcasting System, particularly in public affairs programming (news and political commentary) has always stuck in conservative craws. PBS is 40 percent government-financed through annual "appropriations" passed by Congress, and efforts to de-fund and if possible kill it have been a feature of the political landscape for the past twenty years.

In 1971, President Richard Nixon was furious at the appointment of two "liberals," Sander Vanocur and Robert MacNeil, to anchor a PBS program in Washington; he directed his staff to ensure that "all funds for public broadcasting be cut immediately."[3] Thwarted in this, Nixon's staff decided, in the words of one internal memo, that the best way to "get the left-wing commentators who are cutting us up off public television at once, indeed yesterday if possible" was to stack the board of the controlling body, the Corporation for Public Broadcasting (CPB), with "eight loyalists to control and fire the current staff who make the grants."

This was done by 1972, and both the inquisitiveness and the range of PBS's public-affairs programming nosedived. The new board voted to discontinue funding the networking of all news and political analysis on the PBS system. Conservative political pressures on PBS lightened after Watergate, during Gerald Ford's brief Presidency; and they relaxed during the Carter administration. But Reagan brought them back with redoubled force. On the suppression of PBS, Reagan's ideological stance was exactly the same as Margaret Thatcher's on the BBC. He saw it, essentially, as a rogue cell of liberalism, staffed by malcontents and fellow-travelers—a dirty pinkish-grey blotch on the American Morning, a block to government. Why shouldn't the content of TV be controlled entirely by market forces? A President who had worked for years as a busker on TV for General Electric was not going to pay much attention to arguments about the need for "controversial" programs. In 1981 and again in 1982, Reagan tried (but failed) to get Congress to cancel all federal funding for PBS; learning his lesson, like Nixon before him, he packed the CPB board with conservatives like Richard Brookhiser of *National Review,* and appointed Sonia Landau, who had run a political action committee called "Women For Reagan/Bush" in the 1984 election, as its new chairman. The result of Reagan's intent, as interpreted by the board, was to cast a new chill on current-affairs broadcasting and place PBS more in the hands of corporate sponsorship than it had been before. Corporate underwriters on the whole refused to write checks for current-affairs material, preferring reliable, non-controversial shows like *Masterpiece Theater* or that inexhaustible genre of nature films, electronic wallpaper for the ecologically concerned, known to skeptics in the trade as "bugs fucking to Mozart." There was no way of injecting much liberal "bias" into *those,* since Nature is, from a conservative standpoint, irreproachably competitive in behavior.

Though the conservative campaign for restraint on PBS has a longish history, it has been given a lot of recent impetus by the example of Margaret Thatcher's assault on the independence and funding of the BBC, by competitive-market dogma, and by the religious right. Political and moral reformers, ranging from the Rev. Donald Wildmon to *Commentary* writer David Horowitz, chant in chorus that PBS should be demolished because it's a pinko-liberal-anti-Israel bureaucracy suffused with radical agendas. One wonders how many PBS programs such people have actually watched; PBS's dependence on corporate sponsorship has made it so apolitical or carefully middle-of-the-road that its image as a den of government-subsidized lefties is a joke, especially if you compare its programming content with that of BBC-2 or to Australian, Spanish or French state television.

The conservative Heritage Foundation in Washington has a full time "point man" named Laurence Jarvik, whose job it is to provide ideological ammo for the view that public TV has outlived its use. According to Heritage, there is no worthwhile TV devoted to cultural discussion or political issues that could not be underwritten by American corporations, through an expanding cable system or perhaps some analogue to Great Britain's Channel 4, without using a cent of government money.

Anyone who believes this is (a) dreaming, (b) ignorant of the realities of corporate taste when it sniffs gingerly at program underwriting proposals, or (c) not admitting to his or her agenda. With Heritage, it seems to be a combination of the latter two.

The feasible way to relieve PBS from the onerous fate of being a political football is to finance it, not from annual appropriations by Congress, but with a modest license fee levied on all owners of television sets—as in Great Britain. Or more "radically," as John Wicklein proposed in the *Columbia Journalism Review* in 1986, there could be a 2 percent tax on the profits of commercial broadcasting companies—who enjoy the use of public airways free. This, Wicklein argued, could generate $400 million a year, a sum which "would end the need for direct appropriations, greatly reduce the need for corporate underwriting, and provide the funds necessary for a first-rate national program service." In fact, something very like this has been tried in England, and has proven a resounding creative success—Channel 4, a particular focus of attack from English conservatives. Though Channel 4 was described by Heritage's Laurence Jarvik as "a private commercial channel supported by advertising sales," it is nothing of the kind. It does not depend on direct advertising revenue. It is, in fact, financed by money siphoned from commercial producers on the private channels.

But Niagara will probably run backwards before any such financing systems for non-commercial TV are tried in America—and for two reasons. The first is that Americans, though among the lightest-taxed people on earth, are notoriously resistant to the adage that there is no civilization without taxation. The second is that politicians *want* to retain the appropriations system—it offers control over the content of broadcasting. Just as the far right, at the end of the 80s, wanted to assert moral controls over art.

III

Senator Helms and his allies on the fundamentalist religious right had gone after Mapplethorpe—and Andres Serrano too, and others—for two basic reasons. The first was opportunistic: the need to establish themselves as defenders of the American Way, now that their original crusade against the Red Menace had been rendered null and void by the end of the Cold War and the general collapse of Communism. Having lost the barbarian at the gates, they went for the fairy at the bottom of the garden. But the second reason was that they felt art ought to be morally and spiritually uplifting, therapeutic, a bit like religion. Americans do seem to feel, on some basic level, that the main justification for art is its therapeutic power. That is the basis on which the museums of America have presented themselves to the public ever since they began in the 19th century—education, benefit, spiritual uplift, and not just enjoyment or the recording of cultural history. Its roots are entwined with America's sense of cultural identity as it developed between about 1830 and the Civil War. But they reach down to an earlier soil, that of Puritanism. If we are going to understand what happened at the end of the 80s we have to go back to the very foundations of Protestant America, and not in some facile spirit of ridiculing the Puritan either.

The men and women of 17th-century New England didn't have much time for the visual arts. Painting and sculpture were spiritual snares, best left to the Catholics. Their great source of aesthetic satisfaction was the Word, the *logos*.

In their sermons you glimpse the preoccupations of a later America: the sense of Nature as the sign of God's presence in the world, and the special mission of *American* nature to be this sign and to serve as the metaphor of the good society, new but everlasting, precarious but fruitful. Here is Samuel Sewall (1652–1730), preaching in Massachusetts in 1697, handing down the convenant:

> As long as Plum Island shall faithfully keep the appointed post, notwithstanding all the hectoring words and hard blows of the proud and boisterous ocean; as long as any salmon, or sturgeon, shall swim in the streams of Merrimack . . . as long as any Cattle be fed with the grass growing in the meadows, which do humbly bow themselves down before Turkey Hill; as long as any free and harmless Doves shall find a white oak within the

township, to perch, or feed, or build a careless nest upon . . . *as long as Nature shall not grow old and dote,* but shall constantly remember to give the rows of Indian corn their education, by pairs:—so long shall Christians be born here; and being first made to meet, shall from thence be translated, to be made partakers of the Saints in Light.

Words like Sewall's still have immense resonance for us today. The perception of redemptive nature, which would suffuse 19th-century American painting and reach a climax in our time with the environmental movement, was right there in America from the beginning.

There was as yet no art in America that could rival the spiritual consolations of Nature, or be invested with Nature's moral power. Almost all Americans before 1820 breathed a very thin aesthetic air. They were short of good, let alone great, art and architecture to look at. We tend to forget, when we visit the period rooms of American museums and admire the fine furniture in them that the general aesthetic atmosphere of the early republic was much more like Dogpatch. Most Americans saw no monumental sculpture; few great churches, and none on a European scale of effort and craft; no Colosseums or Pantheons; and as yet, no museums. And everything was new. The public monuments of American classicism, like Jefferson's State Capitol in Virginia, were islands in a sea of far humbler buildings. Average Americans lived not in nice houses with foundations and porches and maybe pediments, still less in permanent edifices of stone or brick, but in makeshift wooden structures that were the ancestors of today's trailer home, only far worse built.

American beauty resided far more in nature than in culture. Thus the intelligent American, if he or she got the chance to visit Europe, could find his taste transformed in a sort of pentecostal flash by a single monument of antiquity, as Jefferson's was by the sight of the Maison Carrée at Nîmes, the Roman temple that created his conception of public architecture. One hour with the Medici Venus in Florence or the Apollo Belvedere in the Vatican could outweigh all one's past aesthetic experience, as the raw child of the new republic. One's own inexperience endowed the English or European work with a stupendous authority.

Today, with mass tourism and mass reproduction to cushion the shock in advance, it is more difficult for us to imagine that state of mind. An American arriving in Europe had no preparation, except maybe from some inaccurate prints, for what he was about to see. To the culturally starved Yankee the arrival in Italy or France seemed like an admission to Heaven, a place reached after an initiation by suffering, the purgatorial voyage across the Atlantic. Four weeks of vomiting, and then . . . Chartres. "We do not dream," one New Yorker wrote in 1845, "of the new sense which is developed by the sight of a masterpiece. It is as though we had always lived in a world where our eyes, though open, saw but a blank, and were then brought into another, where they were saluted by grace and beauty."

IV

To this frame of mind was added a very important component: a general admiration, among the thin ranks of American artlovers, for John Ruskin, whose work began to appear here after 1845. Ruskin never went to America, but he cast a powerful spell over its art-values: you might say that his rolling, supple, irresistible prose afforded the link between (on one hand) the rich ground of religious oratory inherited from the Puritans, and (on the other) the way midcentury Americans were schooling themselves to think about the visual arts and what role they ought to play in a democracy. To overcome Puritan resistance to artificial richness and the sensuous ordering of sight, one had to stress—indeed, wildly exaggerate—the moralizing power of art. You cast your reflections on exalted emotion in religious terms: benefit, conversion, refinement, unification.[4]

Particularly so, since many of the writers were ministers themselves. On their modest tours of Europe they felt art overwhelming them with proof that man was made in God's image, that the soul was immortal, and above all that man-made beauty was part of God's inbuilt design for moral instruction. When Henry Ward Beecher, the top pulpit speaker of his day, went to France to see the cultural sights he spoke of "instant conversion," not mere enjoyment or edification. Of course, one had to choose. One did not like, for instance, Brueghel and Teniers, with all their gorging and puking peasants. One felt somewhat uneasy at the fleshy Madonnas of Titian. Too much model, not enough Virgin. The truly elevating artists were Fra Angelico, the blessed monk of Florence, and of course Raphael. The desire to bring back authoritative spiritual icons of memory naturally condemned the American visitor to disappointment, some of the time. Beecher's sister, Harriet Beecher Stowe, the author of *Uncle Tom's Cabin*, "positively ran," as she recounted it, into the Louvre to find pictures "that would seize and control my whole being. But for such I looked in vain. Most of the men there had painted with dry eyes and cool hearts, thinking little of heroism, faith, love or immortality." The real artist, she went on, went without explanation straight to the heart; his work was not an acquired taste; one did not need to learn to read it.

The idea that it was within the power of the visual arts to change the moral dimension of life reached its peak between the death of Monroe and that of Lincoln. One sees it in full bloom in the weekly editorials in *The Crayon*, New York's main art magazine in the 1850s. It was the voice of the American artist's profession and, as such, held strong views on artists' character and conduct. As the editor bluntly put it in 1855, "The enjoyment of beauty is dependent on, and in ratio with, the moral excellence of the individual. We have assumed that Art is an elevating power, that it has *in itself* a spirit of morality." The first form of the American artist as culture-hero, then, is a preacher. He raised art from being mere craft by moral utterance. God was the supreme artist; they imitated His work, the "Book of Nature." They divided the light and calmed the waters—especially if they were Boston Luminists. They were a counterweight to American materialism.

What was art for?, the *Crayon* asked, in what it called "this hard, angular and grovelling age," the 1850s. Why, it was to show the artist as "a reformer, a philanthropist, full of hope and reverence and love." And if he slipped, he fell a long way, like Lucifer. "If the reverence of men is to be given to Art," warned another editorial, "especial care must be taken that it is not . . . offered in foul and unseemly vessels. We judge religion by the character of its priesthood and we would do well to judge art by the character of those who represent and embody it." One can almost hear the shade of the late Robert Mapplethorpe rustling its leather wings in mirth.

But this proposition, one may be fairly sure, would have been news to most artists—let alone patrons—of the Renaissance. Nobody has ever denied that Sigismondo da Malatesta, the Lord of Rimini, had excellent taste. He hired the most refined of *quattrocento* architects, Leon Battista Alberti, to design a memorial temple to his wife, and then got the sculptor Agostino di Duccio to decorate it, and retained Piero della Francesca to paint it. Yet Sigismondo was a man of such callousness and rapacity that he was known in life as Il Lupo, The Wolf, and so execrated after his death that the Catholic Church made him (for a time) the only man apart from Judas Iscariot officially listed as being in Hell—a distinction he earned by trussing up a Papal emissary, the fifteen-year-old Bishop of Fano, in his own rochet and publicly sodomizing him before his applauding army in the main square of Rimini.

That is not the way trustees of major American cultural institutions are expected to behave. We know, in our heart of hearts, that the idea that people are morally ennobled by contact with works of art is a pious fiction. Some collectors are noble, philanthropic and educated; others are swindling bores who would still think Parmigianino was a kind of cheese if they didn't have the boys at Christie's to set them straight. Museums have been sustained by some of the best and most disinterested people in America, like Duncan Phillips or Paul Mellon; and by some of the worst, like the late Armand Hammer. There is just no generalizing about the moral effects of art, because it doesn't seem to have any. If it did, people who are constantly exposed to it, including all curators and critics, would be saints, and we are not.

V

Under the influence of the Romantic movement, the desire for art as religion changed; it was gradually supplanted by a taste for the Romantic sublime, still morally instructive, but more indefinite and secular. The Hudson River painters created their images of American nature as God's fingerprint; Frederick Church and Albert Bierstadt made immense landscapes that gave Americans all the traits of Romantic art—size, virtuosity, surrender to prodigy and spectacle—except for one: its anxiety. The American wilderness, in their hands, never makes you feel insecure. It is Eden; its God is an American god whose gospel is Manifest Destiny. It is not the world of Turner or Géricault, with its intimations of disaster and death. Nor is it the field of experience that some American *writing* had claimed—Melville's sense of the catastrophic, or Poe's morbid self-enclosure. It is pious, public, and full of uplift.

No wonder it was so popular with the growing American art audience in the 1870s and 1880s. For this audience expected art to grant it relief from the dark side of life. It didn't like either Romantic anguish or realism. There is a strange absence from American painting at this time, like the dog that didn't bark in the night. It is the refusal to deal in any explicit way with the immense social trauma of the Civil War. American art, apart from illustration, hardly mentions the war at all. The sense of pity, fratricidal horror and social waste that pervades the writing of the time, like Walt Whitman, and is still surfacing thirty years later in Stephen Crane's *Red Badge of Courage,* is only to be *seen* in arranged battlefield photographs like those of Mathew Brady—never in painting. This is a curious outcome, particularly if you believe, as I do, that the best strand in 19th-century American art is not so much the Romantic-nationalist one of Bierstadt and Church, but the line of virile, empirical sight that runs from Audubon through Eakins and Homer.

By the 1880s the function of art as quasi-religious uplift was beginning to modulate into a still more secular form, that of art as therapy, personal or social. This deeply affected the character of that special cultural form, the American museum. By now, in its great and growing prosperity, America wanted museums. But they would be different from European ones. They would not, for instance, be stores of imperial plunder, like the British Museum or the Louvre. (Actually, immense quantities of stuff were ripped off from the native Indians and the cultures south of the Rio Grande, but we call this anthropology, not plunder.) They would not be state-run or, except marginally, state-funded. Because state funding, in a democracy, means tax—and since one of the founding myths of America was a tax revolt, the Boston Tea Party, the idea of paying taxes to support culture has never caught on here. Other countries have come, with many a weary groan, to accept the principle that there is no civilization without taxation. Not America, where the annual budget of the National Endowment for the Arts is still around 10 percent of the $1.6 billion the French government set aside for cultural projects in fiscal 1991, and less than our governmental expenditure on military marching bands.

Here, museums would grow from the voluntary decision of the rich to create zones of transcendence within the society; they would share the cultural wealth with a public that couldn't own it. For as the historian Jackson Lears has pointed out in his excellent study of American culture at the 19th century's end, *No Place of Grace,* it is quite wrong to suppose that the Robber Barons (and Baronesses) who were busy applying the immense suction of their capital to the art re-serves of old Europe were doing so from simple greed. Invest-ment hardly figured in their calculations at all—this wasn't the 1980s. Some of them, notably Charles Freer and Isabella Stewart Gardner, were deeply neurasthenic creatures who looked to art to cure their nervous afflictions and thought it could do the same for the less well off. The public museum would soothe the working man—and woman too. The great art of the past would alleviate their resentments. William James put his finger on this in 1903, after he went to the public opening of Isabella Stewart Gardner's private museum in Boston, Fenway Court. He compared it to a clinic. Visiting such a place, he wrote, would give harried self-conscious Americans the chance to forget themselves, to become like children again, immersed in wonder.

The idea that publicly accessible art would help dispel social resentment lay close to the heart of the American mu-seum enterprise. In Europe they thought: well, we already have all these paintings and drawings and sculpture, now let's do something with them: put them in museums. In America they thought: we don't have anything, no art comes with the territory of American identity, so let's acquire art purposively, make it part of what we want to do with a democratic society. We'll refine ourselves along with others. The European mu-seum was by no means indifferent to public education, but the American museum was much more actively concerned with it.

The search for the masterpiece was a vehicle of reconciliation. No other country had sharper cultural contrasts. On one hand, the raw, booming, ruthless, Promethean nature of American capitalism, with the possibility of class war always waiting in the wings. On the other, the idealized past—a past not America's own, but now vicariously within its reach, the Middle Ages and Renaissance that Bernard Berenson and Joseph Duveen were selling to the rich of Boston, Chicago, New York. These were locked together, because one provided relief from the anxieties of the other. Profiting from the Dynamo, Americans now turned to the Virgin; and, as Dorothy Parker jotted in the visitor's book of San Simeon after noticing a Della Robbia over the entrance to Marion Davies's bedroom:

> Upon my honor, I saw a Madonna
> Standing in a niche
> Above the door of the private whore
> Of the world's worst son of a bitch.

America's search for signs of spiritual value in art was not confined to the European Renaissance. It embraced Japan and China too; hence the powerful effect of the so-called Boston bonzes like William Bigelow and Ernest Fenollosa, whose collecting efforts in Japan in search of their own satori would give Boston its unrivaled collection of Japanese art in the 1890s, a time when the Japanese themselves were shedding it off under the early stress of Westernization.

And this emphasis on the therapeutic increased greatly after 1920, between the Armory Show and the time when modernism really started becoming the institutional culture of America. If cultivated American taste resisted modernism at first, it was as much as anything because, in its disjunctiveness and apparent violence to pictorial norms, it didn't seem spiritual enough. Could it deliver on the inherited promise of art, to provide avenues of transcendental escape from the harsh environment of *industrial* modernity? Could you reconcile the Ancients and the Moderns?

The museum answer, right from the moment the Museum of Modern Art was founded, was yes. The American museum had to balance its sober nature against the basic claim of the modernist avant-garde, which is that art advances by injecting doses of unacceptability into its own discourse, thus opening new possibilities of culture. The result was a brilliant adaptation, unheard of in Europe. America came up with the idea of therapeutic avant-gardism, and built museums in its name. These temples stood on two pillars. The first was aestheticism, or art-for-art's sake, which decreed that all works of art should be read first in terms of their formal properties: this freed the art-work from Puritan censure. The second was the familiar one of social benefit: though art-for-art's sake was right to put them outside the frame of moral judgment, works of art were moral in themselves because, whether you knew it or not at first, they pointed the way to higher truths and so did you good. You might be offended at first but then you would adjust, and culture would keep on advancing. Which brings us back to Robert Mapplethorpe's X portfolio, there in the museum.

VI

For the truly amazing thing about the defenses that art-writers made for these scenes of sexual torture is how they were all couched in terms either of an aestheticism that was so solipsistic as to be absurd, or else of labored and unverifiable claims to therapeutic benefit. The first effort depends on a willingness to drag form and content apart that is, quite simply, over the moon. An old acquaintance of mine, dead now, used to relate how she once went in a group around the National Gallery in London led by Roger Fry, the English formalist critic. He stopped to analyze a triptych by Orcagna, featuring God the Father, terrible in his wrath, flashing eyes and streaming beard, pointing implacably to his sacrificed Son. "And now," Fry would say, "we must turn our attention to the dominant central mass." Now, seventy years later, one gets a critic like Janet Kardon, in the Mapplethorpe catalogue and in her testimony in the Cincinnati trial, reflecting on one photo of a man's fist up his partner's rectum, and another of a finger rammed into a penis, and fluting on about "the centrality of the forearm" and how it anchors the composition, and how "the scenes appear to be distilled from real life," and how their formal arrangement "purifies, even cancels, the prurient elements." This, I would say, is the kind of exhausted and literally demoralized aestheticism that would find no basic difference between a Nuremberg rally and a Busby Berkeley spectacular, since both, after all, are examples of Art-Deco choreography. But it is no odder than the diametrically opposite view, advanced by such writers as Ingrid Sischy and Kay Larson—that Mapplethorpe's more sexually extreme images are in some sense didactic: dionysiac in themselves, they have the character of a moral spectacle, stripping away the veils of prudery and ignorance and thus promoting gay rights by confronting us with the outer limits of human sexual behavior, beyond which only death is possible. This, wrote Larson, is "the last frontier of self-liberation and free-dom." The guy with his genitals on the whipping-block be-comes the hip version of the Edwardian mountaineer, dangling from some Himalayan crag: below him the void, around him the rope, and the peak experience above. I find this dubious, to put it mildly. If a museum showed images of such things happening to consenting, masochistic *women,* there would be an uproar of protest from within the art-world: sexism, degradation, exploitation, the lot. What is sauce for the goose is, or should be, sauce for the gander. And in any case, as Rochelle Gurstein pointed out in an excellent piece in *Tikkun,*[5] the Mapplethorpe affair reveals "how many cultural arbiters, like many political theorists, are straitjacketed by a mode of discourse that narrowly con-ceives of disputes over what should appear in public in terms of individual rights—in this case the artist's right of self-expression—rather than in terms that address the public's interest in the quality and character of our modern world." I would defend the exhibition of the X portfolio on First Amendment grounds, as long as it's restricted to consenting adults. But we fool ourselves if we suppose the First Amend-ment exhausts the terms of the debate, or if we go along with the naive idea that all taboos on sexual representation are made to be broken, and that breaking them has some-thing to do with the importance of art, now, in 1992. It is a measure of the heat generated by the Mapplethorpe con-troversy that many of his enthusiasts feel that merely to raise such matters "plays into the hands of" the censorious right.

I have dwelt on the hullaballoo over a part of the work of one somewhat overrated American photographer because it feeds directly into the issue of politics in art, and how American museums treat it. It seems to me that there is absolutely no reason why a museum, any museum, should favor art which is overtly political over art which is not. Today's political art is only a coda to the idea that painting and sculpture can provoke social change.

Throughout the whole history of the avant-garde, this hope has been refuted by experience. No work of art in the 20th century has ever had the kind of impact that *Uncle Tom's Cabin* did on the way Americans thought about slavery, or *The Gulag Archipelago* did on illusions about the real nature of Communism. The most celebrated, widely reproduced and universally recognizable political painting of the 20th century is Picasso's *Guernica,* and it didn't change Franco's regime one inch or shorten his life by so much as one day. What really changes political opinion is events, argument, press photographs, and TV.

The catalogue convention of the 90s is to dwell on activist artists "addressing issues" of racism, sexism, AIDS, and so forth. But an artist's merits are not a function of his or her gender, ideology, sexual preference, skin color or medical condition, and to address an issue is not to address a public. The HIV virus isn't listening. Joe Sixpack isn't looking at the virtuous feminist knockoffs of John Heartfield on the Whitney wall—he's got a Playmate taped on the sheetrock next to the bandsaw, and all the Barbara Krugers in the world aren't going to get him or anyone else to mend his ways. The political art we have in postmodernist America is one long exercise in preaching to the converted. As Adam Gopnik pointed out in the *New Yorker* when reviewing the Carnegie International in Pittsburgh, it consists basically of taking an unexceptionable if obvious idea—"racism is wrong," or "New York shouldn't have thousands of beggars and lunatics on the street"—then coding it so obliquely that when the viewer has re-translated it he feels the glow of being included in what we call the "discourse" of the artworld.[6] But the fact that a work of art is about AIDS or bigotry no more endows it with aesthetic merit than the fact that it's about mermaids and palm trees. And the grotesque exaggeration of some victim-rhetoric can be gauged from the fact that we now have gay activists claiming that homosexuals, of all people, are and, within living memory, have been the victims of bigotry in the American art world. Of all places! In fact, as anyone with the slightest experience of it knows, the art world has long been a refuge for homosexuals, and their "suffering" at its "bigotry" can be gauged from the careers of Robert Rauschenberg, Jasper Johns, Andy Warhol, Ellsworth Kelly, and others too numerous to list. You might as well claim that straight white Protestants are habitually sneered at, snubbed and otherwise tormented in Midwestern country clubs.

In any case, much of the new activist art is so badly made that only its context—its presence in a museum—suggests that it has any aesthetic intention. I know that such an objection cuts no ice with many people: merely to ask that a work of art be well made is, to them, a sign of elitism, and presumably some critics would theorize that a badly made work of art is only a metaphor of how ratty the rest of the world of production has become, now that the ethic of craftsmanship has largely disappeared, so that artistic ineptitude thrust into the museum context has acquired some kind of critical function. But that's not what one really thought when looking at the stuff in the last Whitney Biennial: a sprawling, dull piece of documentation like a school pinboard project by Group

Material called *Aids Timeline,* for instance, or a work by Jessica Diamond consisting of an equals sign canceled out with a cross, underneath which was lettered in a feeble script, "Totally Unequal." Anyone who thinks that this plaintive diagram contributes anything fresh to one's grasp of privilege in America, merely by virtue of getting some wall-space in a museum, is dreaming.

Europe in the last few years has produced a few artists of real dignity, complexity and imaginative power whose work you could call political—Anselm Kiefer, for instance, or Christian Boltanski. But the abiding traits of American victim art are posturing and ineptitude. In the performances of Karen Finley and Holly Hughes you get the extreme of what can go wrong with art-as-politics—the belief that mere expressiveness is enough; that I become an artist by showing you my warm guts and defying you to reject them. You don't like my guts? You and Jesse Helms, fella.

The claims of this stuff are infantile. I have demands, I have needs. Why have you not gratified them? The "you" allows no differentiation, and the self-righteousness of the "I" is deeply anaesthetic. One would be glad of some sign of awareness of the nuance that distinguishes art from slogans. This has been the minimal requirement of good political art, and especially of satire, from the time of Gillray and Goya and Géricault through that of Picasso, John Heartfield and Diego Rivera. But today the stress is on the merely personal, the "expressive." Satire is distrusted as elitist. Hence the discipline of art, indicated by a love of structure, clarity, complexity, nuance and imaginative ambition, recedes; and claims to exemption come forward. I am a victim: how dare you impose your aesthetic standards on me? Don't you see that you have damaged me so badly that I need only display my wounds and call it art? In 1991 there appeared in *Art in America* a gem of an interview with Karen Finley, in which this ex-Catholic performance artist declared that the measure of her oppression as a woman was that she had no opportunity, no chance whatsoever, of becoming Pope. And she meant it. One could hardly find a more vivid epitome of the self-absorption of the artist-as-victim. I am an ex-Catholic myself, and the thought of this injustice struck a chord in me. But mulling it over, I came to see that there is, in fact, a reason why Karen Finley should be ineligible for the Papacy. The Pope is only infallible part of the time, when he is speaking *ex cathedra* on matters of faith and morals. The radical performance artist, in her full status as victim, is infallible all the time. And no institution, not even one as old and cunning as the Catholic Church, could bear the grave weight of continuous infallibility in its leader. This, even more than the prospect of a chocolate-coated Irishwoman whining about oppression on the Fisherman's Throne, is why I should vote against her, if I were a member of the College of Cardinals, which I am not likely to be either.

The pressures of activism are putting a strain on museums, as they are meant to, and they are very quickly internalized by the staff. Two systems of preference about art come into play, and they produce a double censoriousness.

A dramatic example of this happened in Washington in April 1991. The National Museum of American Art put on an exhibition called *The West as America,* a huge anthology of images meant to revise the triumphalist version of the white settlement of America in the 19th century.[7] What did the painters and sculptors of the time tell us about Manifest Destiny? The show began with history-paintings of the Pilgrim Fathers and ended with photos of Californian redwoods with roads cut through their trunks. It was quite frank about choosing works of art as evidence of ideas and opinions, and as records of events, rather than for their intrinsic aesthetic merits. Nothing wrong with that, as long as you make it clear what you're doing, which the curators did. Often quite minor, or aesthetically negligible, or even repellent works of art will tell you a lot about social assumptions. And "masterpieces" are thin on the ground in 19th-century American painting anyhow. What one saw, for the most part, was the earnest efforts of small provincial talents whose work would hardly be worth studying except for the clarity with which it set out the themes of an expansionist America. The show set out to deconstruct images, and this too was fair enough, since if anything in this culture was ever constructed, it is the foundation myth of the American West.

I thought it was an interesting and stimulating show, and said so in a review. What I did not like so much were the catalogue and especially the wall-labels, which were suffused with late-Marxist, lumpen-feminist diatribes. These labels used to be a great feature of Russian museums. "This Fabergé egg, symbol of the frivolous decadence of the Romanoffs . . . ," and so forth. They have vanished from Russia, and migrated here. Here, folks, is a picture of a Huron. Lo, the poor Native American! See, he is depicted as dying! And note the subservient posture of the squaw, an attempt to project the phallocentricity of primitive capitalism onto conquered races! And the broken arrow on the ground, emblem of his lost though no doubt conventionally exaggerated potency! Eeew, gross! Next slide! One of the catalogue authors even turned her attention to the frames around the pictures, claiming that "rectilinear frames . . . provide a dramatic demonstration of white power and control." A little of this goes a long way, and *The West as America* had a lot of it.

Nevertheless I was amazed by the vehemence of the reaction to the show. Starting with Daniel Boorstin, the former Librarian of Congress, a whole crowd of politicos and right-wing columnists put on their boots and started kicking. It occurred to none of them that the legendary history of the American West had been under attack from social historians for years, and that the argument of the Museum's show was neither unprecedented nor particularly new, except insofar as it was transferred into the field of art. Nor did they think it proper that the John Wayne version of the frontier should be questioned at all. And of course the wall-labels played right into their hands. The charge was led by Senator Ted Stevens of Alaska, a Republican pipeliner who had his own reasons for not wanting the Smithsonian to put on shows of what he called "perverted history," that mentioned conquest, development and the fate of Indians. He accused the secretary of the Smithsonian of "having a political agenda," as though he himself did not.

So the message was clear enough: we'll be back, get into line or we'll cut your funds off. This message has filled the ears of American institutions ever since the Mapplethorpe mess. And so the director of the National Museum of American Art, Elizabeth Broun, received quite a lot of goodwill from critics, museum professionals and the like: *The West as America* wasn't a perfect show, it had defects of rhetoric, but it posed real questions about the uses and meanings of American art and seemed, on the balance, well worth doing. And in any case, my enemy's enemy is my friend.

But no sooner had Ms. Broun emerged from the murk

of rightwing censoriousness, than she decided to do a little correcting of her own. The month after the *West* show closed, the NMAA opened another, organized by another museum and traveling to Washington, which contained a work by the noted American miniimalist Sol LeWitt. LeWitt is mainly known for his modular grids, but this work was an early one from the 1960s—a box into which one looked at images, repetitious serial enlargements of a full-frontal photo of a naked woman. In a transport of political correctness Ms. Broun decided that Mr. LeWitt was causing the viewer to focus in a prurient and sexist manner on the lady's pubic bush, and forthwith banned the work from the show. The curator who'd put the LeWitt in there in the first place immediately launched a press campaign, alleging censorship; the work was put back. Good censorship—no, let us call it intervention-based affirmative sensitivity—is therapeutic and redounds to the advantage of women and minorities. Bad censorship is what the pale penis people do to you. Here endeth the lesson.

VII

Am I alone in finding something rather narrow-minded and stultifying about this? Clearly not: political pressures have in the last few years become a grim encumbrance for American museums, and a topic of obsessive worry for their professional staff. There is a right jaw of the vise, and a left one, and between the two the museum is painfully squeezed and may in the end be distorted out of useful shape. These pressures are far more extreme in the United States than in any European country I know of. They are the result of a totalization of political influence, a belief—common to both left and right—that no sphere of public culture should be exempt from political pressure, since everything in it supposedly boils down to politics anyway. This is the outcome both of the PC belief that the personal is the political, acts of imagination not exempted, and of the conservative view that any stick that you can beat liberals with is a good stick, and never mind what else gets flattened in the struggle. The American museum was never designed to be an arena for such disputes, and thus is proving decidedly awkward and even inept at responding to them. And its response is complicated by the claims of activist art to constitute an avant-garde.

For the last quarter-century it has also been obvious that the idea of an avant-garde corresponds to no cultural reality in America. Its myth, that of the innovative artist or group struggling against an entrenched establishment, is dead. Why? Because new art has formed our official culture ever since we can remember. America is addicted to progress; it loves the new as impartially as it loves the old. Hence the idea of an avant-garde could only survive here as a fiction, supported by devotional tales of cultural martyrdom; the context of these tales has now moved from style to gender and race, but the plot remains much the same. Today, nobody uses the term "avant-garde" any more—it's a nonword. Instead, dealers and curators say "cutting edge," which still conveys the warmly positivist impression of hot new stuff slicing through the reactionary opposition, leaving the old stuff behind, shaping something, forging ahead.

Unfortunately this model was trashed in the 80s and cannot be revived. The idea of therapeutic soulcraft through art sank when the artworld became the art industry, when the greed and glitz of the Reagan era started riding on that "cutting edge," when thousands of speculators got into the market and the junk-bond mentality hit contemporary art. As the artworld filled up with sanctimonious folk who under other circumstances would have been selling swamp in Florida or snake-oil in Texas, the more elevated its language became. Every asset-stripper with a Salle on his wall could prattle knowingly of hyper-reality and commodification. You cannot have an orgy like the 80s without a hangover, and now we have a big one. The population of the artworld expanded enormously in the 80s, thanks to overproduction of art school degrees in the 70s and the sudden lure of the market. No conceivable base of collectors was large enough to support them, not even in the seven fat years that ended with the art market crash of 1990, let alone in the lean years that presumably lie ahead. Since the decay of American art education has been steady for the last three decades, most of them, like most people who do creative writing courses, are ill-trained and unlikely to produce anything memorable. It's not their fault: the art education system let them down by promoting theory over skill, therapy over apprenticeship, strategies over basics. In an overpopulated artworld with a depressed market, you are going to hear more and more about how artists are discriminated against—endless complaints about racism, sexism and so on; whereas the real problem is that there are too many artists for the base to support. There are probably 200,000 artists in America, and assuming that each of them makes forty works a year, that yields eight million objects, most of which don't have a ghost of a chance of survival. Maybe what we need is a revival of the WPA projects of the 1930s, not that there's the slightest likelihood of that. But certainly most of this surplus and homeless work isn't going to find a home in the museum.

The sense of disenfranchisement among artists has led to a stream of attacks on the idea of "quality," as though it were the enemy of justice. These, above all, the serious museum must resist. We have seen what they have done to academic literary studies. Quality, the argument goes, is a plot. It is the result of a conspiracy of white males to marginalize the work of other races and cultures. To invoke its presence in works of art is somehow inherently repressive.

A great deal of conventionalized complaint has been spun around this thesis. It has become the New Orthodoxy and, to an increasing degree, art critics and art historians seem unable to resist it. As one example from a possible myriad, consider this passage from an essay by Eunice Lipton, in the catalogue to the exhibition called THE DECADE SHOW, held jointly at the Museum of Contemporary Hispanic Art, the Studio Museum in Harlem and the New Museum of Contemporary Art in New York in 1990. "One of the most powerful ways art history produces insiders and outsiders," Lipton writes,[8]

> is through its notion of "artist-geniuses" . . . Near-requirements for this artist-hero are his impassioned tirades, his Old Testament fervor, his uncontrollable sexual drives, his competitiveness (set on the stage of Freud's Oedipal complex), and most of all, his single-minded obsession with work. Just think about Michelangelo, van Gogh, Rodin, Picasso, Pollock. Could these artists be lesbians, Asian Americans, Native Americans? White discourse shudders to contemplate such chaos, so potent a threat do these transgressions pose.

Well, I suppose that the first answer to Ms. Lipton's burning question is: No, these artists couldn't be other than what

they were, because, for a start, they are all dead. No effort of
the imagination—or none that makes any sense—is going to
give van Gogh a Chinese mother, or turn Rodin into a Chero-
kee: it is too late for them to undergo such "transgressive"
changes, no matter how desirable the project may seem to
critics like Ms. Lipton. At least Michelangelo was homosexual,
if not a full-fledged lesbian, though I guess this doesn't get
his admirers off the hook. But the remarkable thing about
this passage is, I think, the way in which it sets up a caricature
of what Ms. Lipton calls "white discourse." Her description
of modern art history's idea of the Romantic artist-hero is an
Aunt Sally, a crude pasteboard effigy which no art historian
uses and no serious critic would do more than laugh at. It is
a journalistic fiction—and low-grade journalism at that. The
stereotype of the artist as a sort of phallocratic demiurge,
creating arbitrary marvels in a social void, continues to have
an appeal to mass culture, but it's Judith Krantz's territory,
not art history's. Anyone with half a grain of sense knows that
to get to Michelangelo we have to start by getting past the
picture drawn of him in *The Agony and the Ecstasy,* and that
Lust for Life is not where you begin if you want to grasp
something about van Gogh. And has anyone ever written
about Chardin in terms of his "uncontrollable sexual drives,"
or Piero della Francesca in terms of his "Old Testament fer-
vor," or Watteau's "impassioned tirades"?

Actually, it now seems that the pseudo-heroics and bio-
graphical panting that critics like Lipton deplore in the treatment of the likes of Michelangelo or van Gogh, however
repressive and hegemonic when applied to whites, are positively desirable for blacks. Such "reinforcement" criticism is
now increasingly fashionable in America. It's bad to use words

like "genius" *unless* you are talking about the late Jean-Michel Basquiat, the black Chatterton of the 80s who, during a picturesque career as sexual hustler, addict and juvenile art-star, made a superficial mark on the cultural surface by folding the conventions of street graffiti into those of *art brut* before killing himself with an overdose at the age of twenty-seven. The first stage of Basquiat's fate, in the mid-80s, was to be effusively welcomed by an art industry so trivialized by fashion and blinded by money that it couldn't tell a scribble from a Leonardo. Its second stage was to be dropped by the same audience, when the novelty of his work wore off. The third was an attempt at apotheosis four years after his death, with a large retrospective at the Whitney Museum designed to sanitize his short frantic life and position him as a kind of all-purpose, inflatable martyr-figure, thus restoring the dollar value of his *oeuvre* in a time of collapsing prices for American contemporary art. In the course of this solemn exercise in Heroic Victimology, all the hyperbole of the artist-as-demi-urge was revived. One contributor to the catalogue proclaimed that "Jean remains wrapped in the silent purple toga of Immortality"; another opined that "he is as close to Goya as American painting has ever produced." A third, not to be outdone, extolled Basquiat's "punishing regime of self-abuse" (*sic*) as part of "the disciplines imposed by the principle of inverse asceticism to which he was so resolutely committed." These disciplines of inverse asceticism, one sees, mean shooting smack until you drop dead. The kid died for *your* sins. Through addiction, wrote a fourth catalogue essayist, Basquiat "parodied, and sought to heal a disturbed culture." As if this cultural Newspeak wasn't enough, one had the opinion of the Whitney's director, David Ross: "Racial and ethnic division remains a central problem in American life, and lingering racist presumptions seriously cloud the ability of many to understand Basquiat." You cannot "understand" him, apparently, and still find him trivial; hence, by wetly-breathing implication, if you don't love Basquiat's work, it's because you hate blacks. It is a sign of our times that a major New York museum could resort to such emotional bribery.[9]

Lurking behind this drivel is a barely concealed longing for cultural segregation. It corresponds to one of the most corrosive currents in the American polity today—corrosive, I mean, to any idea of common civic ground—which is to treat the alleged cultural and educational needs of groups (women, blacks, Latinos, Chinese-Americans, gays, you name it) as though they overrode the needs of any individual and were all, automatically, at odds with the allegedly monolithic desires of a ruling class, alternately fiendish and condescending, of white male heterosexual capitalists. More and more, it is assumed that one's cultural reach is fixed and determined forever by whatever slot one is raised in. One can imagine the contempt with which a great Mexican artist like Diego Rivera would have reacted to this. Rivera never thought he was "not empowered," and neither did Frida Kahlo, although God knows she fitted every category of outsiderhood in the current litany of complaint: a bisexual *Latina* who spent most of her life in severe physical pain. Rivera probably gave more to Mexico, in terms of self-knowledge and cultural pride, than any artist in its history, but he was only able to do so because he had absorbed and completely internalized the great tradition of Renaissance fresco-painting, which combined with his absorption in French modernism, pre-Columbian Mexican art and living folk-art to produce the tremendous results we see on the walls of the Palacio Nacional in Mexico City. If you had told Rivera that quality didn't matter, he would have laughed in your face.

Now you can't deny that, at any time in the history of art, there have been inflated reputations and wrongly ignored artists. That happens in the short term, but in the long term the injustices tend to be corrected. Twenty years ago, the American art system was wholly phallocratic. Today there remains little institutional bias against women artists, probably even less than there is against female writers or editors in American publishing. Against blacks there is more, but even that is rapidly fading.

Part of the hangover of the 80s, however, is the vertigo that comes when you realize how many of the eagles of the time were turkeys. The cultural feeding frenzy was hard on artists who develop slowly, on those who value a certain classical reticence and a precise accountancy of feeling over mere expressiveness or contestation. It also presented difficulties for those who believe that art based on the internal traditions of painting and sculpture may achieve values which simply aren't accessible to art based on mass media. In some ways, such people face barriers of taste and museum practice today that are quite as formidable as the crust of received ideas a century ago. The American artworld is in gridlock today. Its museum curators are still in thrall to the market; its supposed variety is a myth, since it clings to the 80s star-system; its institutions march in lockstep, imposing a uniformity of taste that has few parallels in American cultural history.

And now, the cherry on this stale cultural sundae is that artists must contend with the deadening sentimentality that

American-style institutional multiculturalism breeds. Those who talk about multiculturalism as a "radical" program fail to see how conventionalizing, soothing and altogether consoling to middlebrow taste its effects on art may turn out to be. This is already visible in one area: that of publicly funded art, where "multicultural" programs serve to get the embattled National Endowment for the Arts off the hook of making any discriminations at all. If the philistines are baying for an end to government support to "high"—which is to say, difficult and possibly controversial—art; if the moralists are yelling for the blood of any poet or performer whose work doesn't accord with "family values" and might raise hackles in some golf-club in Tulsa—then what could be a better refuge than remedial multiculturalism? Just turn the already meager trickle of government money towards stuff that nobody could quarrel with: "Hmong needlework, coastal sea-grass basketry, southeast Alaska native dance, American Indian basketry and woodcraft, Pacific Island canoe building, and Appalachian banjo-playing," to quote from a recent brochure issued by the NEA to show just how warm and cuddly the relation of government to nostalgically valued pockets of local culture has become after the *tsuris* of Mapplethorpe and Serrano. Is anyone going to bash the NEA for subsidizing some village craftsman outside Seattle to form a "community outreach program" in order to inculcate "self-esteem" in schoolchildren by showing them how to carve Kwakiutl-style beavers in cedar? Of course not. Multiculturalism and "cultural diversity," as interpreted by federal funding agencies and an increasing number of private foundations, shade over into pious hobbyism. They produce little that might, in aesthetic terms, challenge, refine, criticize or in any way extend the thinking of the status quo. They are designed to appease a populist mentality that contents itself with the easy task of "supporting ethnicity and gender differences in the arts" instead of the hard one of looking for real excellence. Most of the "art" that results from such programs is affirmative, prolix kitsch. People like it for much the same reasons that they like Hallmark cards with *sumi-e* herons and New Age verses on them. It just makes them feel . . . good. You can certainly run a feelgood cultural program on sociological and statistical criteria, backing it up with the usual pieties about "empowerment." This conforms very well to the evangelical tradition of American cultural life—the idea that one is morally improved, uplifted, turned into a better citizen, by either producing or consuming art. But the art it fosters may be, and often is, quite banal. Populist multiculturalism can also swiftly turn into a form of reverse racism, as any white male artist who has lately applied for a grant in southern California now knows. What happens where government arts money and populist multiculturalism intersect? Moral blackmail, with one gimlet eye on the pork-barrel.

This might not matter if government gave lots of money to the arts, so that everyone got a share. But as is well known, government does no such thing. The American pork-barrel is not full. It is more like a sandwich bag. The American taxpayer contributes $0.68 to the support of the arts every year, compared to $27 in Germany and $32 in France. In Holland for the last twenty years they tried populist pork for everyone. The government set up a fund to buy work by artists almost irrespective of how good it was. All that mattered was that they should be alive and Dutch. About 8,000 Dutch artists are represented in that collection. None of it is shown and as everyone in Holland except the artists involved now admits, about 98 percent of it is rubbish. The artists think it's all junk except their own work. The storage, air-conditioning and maintenance expenses are now so high that they have to get rid of the stuff. But they can't. Nobody wants it. You can't give it away. They tried giving it to public institutions, like lunatic asylums and hospitals. But even the lunatic asylums insisted on standards—they wanted to pick and choose. So there it all sits, democratic, non-hierarchical, non-elitist, non-sexist, unsalable and, to the great regret of the Dutch government, only partially biodegradable.

Now there are lessons from this. The first is that if Dutch lunatic asylums can discriminate about art without being accused of antidemocratic elitism, so can American museums. Democracy's task in the field of art is to make the world safe for elitism. Not an elitism based on race or money or social position, but on skill and imagination. The embodiment of high ability and intense vision is the only thing that makes art popular. Basically, it's why the Rijksmuseum is full of people and the remedial art-basements of Amsterdam are not. The greatest popular spectacles in America are elitist to the core: football games, baseball games, basketball, professional tennis. But nobody is going to pay to watch Hilton Kramer and me swim the 800-meter freestyle in 35 minutes flat, despite our privileged position as not-quite-dead white European males. Like sport, art is an area in which elitism can display itself at a negligible cost in social harm.

The second lesson is that if a scrupulous participatory democracy like Holland spends twenty-five times per taxpayer what America does on culture, choosing art on sociological grounds in the name of complete cultural egalitarianism, and ends up with a garbage-disposal problem, what guarantee is there that we can do any better here? None, that I can see.

It is in the nature of human beings to discriminate. We make choices and judgments every day. These choices are part of real experience. They are influenced by others, of course, but they are not fundamentally the result of a passive reaction to authority. And we know that one of the realest experiences in cultural life is that of inequality between books and musical performances and paintings and other works of art. Some things do strike us as better than others—more articulate, more radiant with consciousness. We may have difficulty saying why, but the experience remains. The pleasure principle is enormously important in art, and those who would like to see it downgraded in favor of ideological utterance remind me of the English Puritans who opposed bear-baiting, not because it gave pain to the bear, but because it gave pleasure to the spectators.

For instance, my hobby is carpentry. I am fair at it—for an amateur. That is to say, I can make a drawer that slides, and do kitchen cabinets to a tolerance of about three thirty-seconds of an inch, not good enough to be really good, but fair. I love the tools, the smell of shavings, the rhythm of work. I know that when I look at a Hepplewhite cabinet in a museum, or a frame house in Sag Harbor, I can read it—figure its construction, appreciate its skills—better than if I had never worked wood myself. But I also know that the dead hands that made the breakfront or the porch were far better than mine; they ran finer mouldings, they knew about expansion, and their veneer didn't have bumps. And when I see the level of woodworking in a Japanese structure like the great temple of Horyu-ji, the precision of the complex joints, the understanding of *hinoki* cypress as a live substance, I know that I couldn't do anything like that if I had my whole life to live over. People who can make such things are an elite; they have earned the right to be. Does this fill me, the woodbutcher whose joints meet at 89 or 91 degrees, with resentment? Absolutely not. Reverence and pleasure, more like.

Mutatis mutandis, it's the same in writing and in the visual arts. You learn to discriminate. Not all cats are the same in the light. After a while you can see, for instance, why a drawing by Pater or Lancret might be different from one of exactly the same subject by Watteau: less tension in the line, a bit of fudging and fussing, and so on. This corresponds to experience, just as our perception and comparison of grace in the work of a basketball player or a tennis pro rise from experience. These differences of intensity, meaning, grace can't be set forth in a little catechism or a recipe-book. They can only be experienced and argued, and then seen in relation to a history that includes social history. If the museum provides the ground for this, it is doing its job. If it does not—and one of the ways of not doing it is to get distracted by problems of displaced ideology—then it is likely to fail, no matter how warm a glow of passing relevance it may feel. Likewise, museum people serve not only the public but the artist, *whether that artist's work is in the collection or not,* by a scrupulous adherence to high artistic and intellectual standards. This discipline is not quantifiable, but it is or should be disinterested, and there are two sure ways to wreck it. One is to let the art market dictate its values to the museum. The other is to convert it into an arena for battles that have to be fought— but fought in the sphere of politics. Only if it resists both can the museum continue with its task of helping us discover a great but always partially lost civilization: our own.

Notes

Lecture 1

1. See Cathy Young, "Victimhood Is Powerful: Both Feminists and Antifeminists See Advantages in Keeping Women Down," *Reason,* October 1992.

2. Nat Hentoff, "What Really Happened at Betty's Oceanview Diner," *Village Voice,* January 7, 1992.

3. See Adam Redfield, letter to *New York Times* dated 11/22/91.

4. Barbara Ehrenreich, in *Democratic Left,* July/Aug. 1991; repr. in Paul Berman (ed.), *Debating P.C., The Controversy over College Political Correctness on Campuses,* 1992, p. 336.

5. Reported by William Henry III, "Upside Down in the Groves of Academe," *Time,* 4/1/1991.

6. Nat Hentoff, " 'Speech Codes' on the Campus and Problems of Free Speech," *Dissent,* Fall 1991, p. 546.

7. Ibid., p. 549.

8. Tom Wicker, "The Democrats as the Devil's Disciples," *New York Times*, 8/30/92.

9. Michael Thomas, "The Money Game," catalogue introduction to *Culture and Commentary, An Eighties Perspective*, Hirshhorn Museum, 1990, p. 147.

10. William Greider, *Who Will Tell the People: The Betrayal of American Democracy*, 1992, p. 25.

11. Seymour Martin Lipset and Earl Raab, *The Politics of Unreason: Right-Wing Extremism in America, 1790–1970*, p. 103.

12. Ibid., p. 114.

13. Ibid., p. 239.

14. See Berman (ed.), Introduction to *Debating P.C.*, 1992.

15. Carol Gruber, *Mars and Minerva: World War I and the Uses of Higher Learning in America*; William Summerscales, *Affirmation and Dissent: Columbia's Response to the Crisis of World War I*; both cited by Cyrus Veeser, in a letter to the *New York Times*, 6/23/91.

16. Daniel J. Singal, "The Other Crisis in American Education," *The Atlantic Monthly*, Nov. 1991, p. 67.

17. Eugene Genovese, "Heresy, Yes—Sensitivity, No," *New Republic*, 4/15/91.

18. Louis Menand, "Lost Faculties," *New Republic*, 7/9/90.

19. Gerald Graff, *Literature Against Itself*, Chicago, 1979, pp. 96–97.

20. Daniel Harris, "Make My Rainy Day," *The Nation*, 6/8/92.

Lecture 2

1. Andrew Riemer, *Inside Outside* (Sydney, 1992), p. 157.

2. Les Murray, "The Human-Hair Thread," in *Persistence in Folly: Selected Prose Writings* (Sydney, 1984), p. 4.

3. David Rieff, *Making Sense of Multiculturalism*, unpublished essay, 1992.

4. Katha Pollitt, "Canon to the Right of Me . . ." *The Nation,* 9/23/91.

5. Frederick Crews, Introduction to *The Critics Bear It Away: American Fiction and the Academy,* New York, 1992, p. xv.

6. Edward Saïd, "The Politics of Knowledge," *Raritan,* Summer 1991.

7. Jorge Amado, "El embeleso colonial." *El Pais,* 8/23/92.

8. The "African-American Baseline Essays," in reprint form, are obtainable from Supt. Matthew Prophet, Portland Public Schools, 501 N. Dixon St., Portland, OR 97227.

9. Cheikh Anta Diop, *Civilization or Barbarism: An Authentic Anthropology,* New York 1991. Originally published as *Civilisation ou Barbarie,* Paris, 1981.

10. Basil Davidson, *Africa in History,* London, 1984 ed., p. 38.

11. Diop, *Civilization or Barbarism,* Introduction, p. 3.

12. For a leading black scholar's summary and rebuttal of the "new anti-Semitism" in Afrocentrist circles, see Henry Louis Gates, Jr., "Black Demagogues and Pseudo-Scholars," *New York Times,* 7/20/92.

13. David Brian Davis, *Slavery and Human Progress,* Ithaca, 1984, p. 33.

14. See Harold Brackman, *Farrakhan's Reign of Historical Error: The Truth Behind "The Secret Relationship Between Blacks and Jews,"* Simon Wiesenthal Center Reports, 1992.

15. See Roland Oliver, *The African Experience,* London 1991, especially—for a discussion of enslavement of Africans by Africans—chapter 10, "Masters and Slaves," *passim.*

16. Eric Hobsbawm (ed.) et al., *The Invention of Tradition,* Cambridge, 1983.

Lecture 3

1. Richard Bolton, Introduction to *Culture Wars: Documents from the Recent Controversies in the Arts,* New York, 1992, p. 9.

2. Healey's testimony: ibid., p. 130 ff.

3. John Wicklein, "The Assault on Public Television," *Columbia Journalism Review,* Jan./Feb. 1986, pp. 27–29. The Nixon memo was released in 1979 under the Freedom of Information Act.

4. For the evangelical background to American art-appreciation in the 19th century the most valuable discussion, on which I have drawn heavily here, is Neil Harris, *The Artist in American Society: The Formative Years, 1790–1860,* Chicago, 1966.

5. Rochelle Gurstein, "Misjudging Mapplethorpe: The Art Scene and the Obscene," *Tikkun,* Nov./Dec. 1991.

6. Adam Gopnik, "Empty Frames," *New Yorker,* 11/25/91.

7. See catalogue to William Truettner (ed.), *The West as America: Reinterpreting Images of the Frontier, 1820–1920,* with essays by Nancy K. Anderson . . . [et al.], Smithsonian Institution, 1991.

8. See Eunice Lipton, "Here Today, Gone Tomorrow? Some Plots for a Dismantling," in catalogue to *The Decade Show: Frameworks of Identity in the 1980s,* New York, 1990.

9. See, *passim,* catalogue to *Jean-Michel Basquiat,* Whitney Museum, New York, 1992.